SPECIAL PRAISE

for

Cured

"Doctors are human, but at times studying to become a doctor requires super-human efforts. In her new memoir that reads like an engrossing novel, Dr. Anne McTiernan highlights the challenges of combining medical school with motherhood. It's a page-turner!"

—Mikhail "Doctor Mike" Varshavski, DO
Family physician, #1 Health/Medicine influencer
with 10,000,000+ followers

"In *Cured*, Dr. Anne McTiernan peels back the polished veneer of the accomplished physician scientist to reveal an achingly human, wise, and kind woman with whom we can all identify."

—Kathryn Schmitz, PhD, MPH
Professor of Public Health Sciences, Penn State College of Medicine
and past President, American College of Sports Medicine

"*Cured: A Doctor's Journey from Panic to Peace* is a book that speaks to all of us who've feared our dreams are out of reach. Dr. McTiernan tells an engaging and powerful story that will surely inspire many to overcome their fears to accomplish their loftiest goals."

—Theo Pauline Nestor
Author of How to Sleep Alone in a King-Size Bed *and* Writing Is My Drink

"For anyone needing inspiration for overcoming adversity, *Cured* is the book for you. Dr. Anne McTiernan shares her life experiences with probing honesty, keen insight, and humor. This is ultimately a story of resilience, survivorship, and the power of the human spirit."

—JoAnn E. Manson, MD, DrPH,
Professor of Medicine, Harvard Medical School
Chief of Preventive Medicine, Brigham and Women's Hospital
Boston, Massachusetts

"A fascinating look at the making of a physician. Dr. McTiernan's story is full of extraordinary ups, agonizing downs, and remarkable moments of self-discovery. This book is as real as it gets. I couldn't put it down."

—Matt McCarthy, MD,
Author of Superbugs: The Race to Stop an Epidemic,
Assistant Professor of Medicine, Weill-Cornell Medicine

CURED

ANNE McTIERNAN

Cured

A Doctor's Journey from
Panic to Peace

A Memoir

CENTRAL RECOVERY PRESS

Las Vegas

Central Recovery Press (CRP) is committed to publishing exceptional materials addressing addiction treatment, recovery, and behavioral healthcare topics.

For more information, visit www.centralrecoverypress.com.

Publisher: Central Recovery Press
3321 N. Buffalo Drive
Las Vegas, NV 89129

26 25 24 23 22 21   1 2 3 4 5

Library of Congress Cataloging-in-Publication Data

Title: Cured : a doctor's journey from panic to peace : a memoir / Anne
    McTiernan.
Description: Las Vegas, NV : Central Recovery Press, [2020] | Summary: "A
    trailblazing physician and health researcher shares her journey of
    resilience and self-awakening"—Provided by publisher.
Identifiers: LCCN 2020015984 (print) | LCCN 2020015985 (ebook) | ISBN
    9781949481389 (paperback) | ISBN 9781949481396 (ebook)
Subjects: LCSH: McTiernan, Anne—Mental health. | Physicians—United
    States—Diaries.
Classification: LCC R154.M35 A3 2020 (print) | LCC R154.M35 (ebook) | DDC
    610.92 [B]--dc23
LC record available at https://lccn.loc.gov/2020015984
LC ebook record available at https://lccn.loc.gov/2020015985

Photo of Anne McTiernan by Susie Fitzhugh.

Every attempt has been made to contact copyright holders. If copyright holders have not been properly acknowledged please contact us. Central Recovery Press will be happy to rectify the omission in future printings of this book.

Publisher's Note
This book contains general information about mental health, anxiety, panic attacks, and related matters. The information contained herein is not medical advice. This book is not an alternative to medical advice from your doctor or other professional healthcare provider.

Our books represent the experiences and opinions of their authors only. Every effort has been made to ensure that events, institutions, and statistics presented in our books as facts are accurate and up-to-date. To protect their privacy, the names of some of the people, places, and institutions in this book may have been changed.

Cover design and interior by Marisa Jackson.

TO MARTIN, CASSANDRA, AND RACHEL

Contents

ACKNOWLEDGMENTS

This book exists thanks to many people. Some taught me to be a healer, some helped me heal, and others guided me as I wrote my narrative.

First, I thank my husband Martin, who encouraged me throughout the development of this book. Most importantly, he allowed his story to appear on these pages. The book would not have its emotional depth without his inclusion. He also read several drafts, performed excellent editing, and gave me suggestions on how to improve clarity.

I thank also our two beautiful daughters, Rachel and Cassandra, and their wonderful families for tolerating my life-baring narrative. I thank them for allowing themselves to appear in this book. They really were the adorable children I wrote about. Throughout my medical training, they helped me to ground myself in the present and avoid fretting about the past or fearing the future. Their children—Esme, Martin, and Isaac—now do the same for their Grandma.

I am grateful to my wise agent, Anne Devlin, for her continued encouragement and support. I give special thanks to Nancy Schenck for shaping and improving the book. Special thanks also to Valerie Killeen and John Davis for believing in the book and continuing to include me in the Central Recovery Press family and to Patrick Hughes for his guidance in helping *Cured* reach a wide audience.

My first creative writing teacher, Theo Nestor, taught me the art and science of memoir. Her influence shows throughout this book and its predecessor, *Starved: A Nutrition Doctor's Journey from Empty to Full* (Central Recovery Press, 2016). Jennifer D. Munro, my developmental editor and mentor, helped me see the big picture in *Cured*. She also performed brilliant word surgery as she edited this book.

I thank the many family members, friends, and colleagues who have encouraged me as I wrote this memoir. I am indebted to Deborah, Frank, Jenny, and Marcia for helping me to grow emotionally. Finally, I am eternally grateful to Jack, who helped me out of an anxious abyss and taught me to feel rather than fear.

AUTHOR'S NOTE

This book is a memoir; and, as such, reflects my memory of events during my medical training and earlier life. I reconstructed conversations from memory; these may differ from other people's memories. In some cases, I created dialogue to support the narrative. The names and characteristics of my immediate family are real, but I have changed the names and physical characteristics of many other people in the book to preserve their privacy. The patients I wrote about are based on composites of patients. While I cared for individuals with the diseases I describe, the exact characteristics of the patients I describe do not correspond to my actual patients. I did this to preserve their privacy, and to follow legal and good clinical practice guidelines.

Prologue

AUGUST 1985

Valhalla, New York

Dead bodies surrounded me. They lay on their backs, supine in medical terminology. I imagined some staring at the white plastic sheets that covered them completely, others glaring at their closed eyelids. Their smell, a mixture of formaldehyde and death, made me gag.

I was no stranger to the deceased. I'd met many of my Irish-American relatives at Catholic wakes and funerals, which were more family parties than bereavement rites. Yet corpses horrified me. They represented the end of life, separation from loved ones, the possibility of a soul's eternal damnation. Now as a first-year medical student in introductory anatomy lab, I would examine and touch a cadaver daily to learn the mysteries of the human body. I was thirty-two years old, but terrified that these corpses would drag me into their netherworld.

My life before that day was full, yet I felt empty. Married for nine years, mother to seven-year-old and three-year-old girls, and recently awarded a PhD in public health, I was successful on the surface. But I'd always felt inadequate, not fully formed. I'd hoped that studying Medicine would make me a powerful woman, would help me feel okay about myself. I had fooled the admissions committee at New York

Medical College into accepting me. On my application essay, I'd written that I wanted to save others. In truth, I was trying to save myself.

I hoped to join the exalted club of physicians, healers, and holders of the secrets to long and healthy lives. But, raised as an Irish-American Catholic by a single mother, with no father in my life, I felt better prepared to be a maid than a doctor, more suited to be a nun than wife and mother.

Now, as I leaned against the wall of the anatomy lab, my vision dimmed. Everything turned gray. I gulped for air. My arms and legs went numb. I felt that drowning sensation I'd had in third grade when a nun pushed my head between my legs. Or like the time when I was eight months pregnant and took a hot shower at the university gym. I prayed that I wouldn't pass out on my first day of medical school classes. I didn't want those MDs-to-be, all smarter and younger than me, to know I couldn't handle this, that I didn't belong.

I pressed harder against the white wall, willing myself to remain upright with the living rather than supine with the corpses. Little did I know that the enormity of medical school would soon wash over me, causing these drowning-like symptoms to occur over and over again, until I reached out for help.

Chapter 1

It all began three years before, in Seattle.

I sat alone in the middle of the long side of a steel conference table. My five inquisitors sat opposite me. The sweat forming on my forehead and underarms bothered me but not as much as the wetness under the front of my blouse. I had made the mistake of thinking about my three-month-old baby, hoping she was taking the bottle okay from her dad. Just one mental image of her was enough to trigger my milk let-down reflex. I wasn't sure if my homemade breast pads could hold the deluge. My breasts didn't care that I was in the middle of my University of Washington PhD dissertation defense.

With mouth dry and pulse bounding, I'd just given a presentation of my epidemiologic study on thyroid cancer in women. Four years of painstaking courses, exams, research, data collection, analyses, and writing, boiled down to thirty minutes. Now, I was answering questions fired at me by the faculty members—four males and one female—who had the power to grant or deny me this prestigious degree. To the twenty-nine-year old me, they seemed like ancient and powerful holders of wisdom. In reality, they were forty-something mid-career academics: my PhD supervisor who was an eminent epidemiologist, a cancer epidemiologist, a thyroid doctor, a statistician, and a female epidemiologist who received fewer accolades and probably lower pay than the rest of them. One by one, each of the professors asked about the study methods and results, and how I might design a better study in the future. After the committee grilled me for an hour, during which time they each showed their own superior knowledge, they told me to wait outside while they deliberated my fate.

Thankful to escape, I sat down on a folding metal chair outside the conference room in the antechamber to the School of Public Health's dean's office. This was not the plush, oak-paneled dean's office of an Ivy League school. Rather, the utilitarian, government-office décor was in various shades of gray. Not a good color choice for Seattle with its perennial steel-hued skies. I shivered, my sweat now evaporating in the typical cool June air and tried not to imagine my dissertation committee deciding that I'd never make it as an independent scientist or that I'd need at least another year's work or that my research was fatally flawed.

I couldn't fail. Academics was the only thing I'd ever excelled at. If I failed, I had nothing to fall back on. No Plan B. Other than my extended schooling, all of my positions had been menial: hotel maid, doughnut waitress, ice cream shop server, telephone operator, file clerk. I couldn't afford to take any of those jobs—I'd have to spend more in day care costs than they would pay.

My anxiety kept me from feeling as exhausted as I should have been, given the lack of sleep the previous night. Our baby daughter, who slept between my husband and me in our double bed, had decided to nurse all night long. By morning, one breast looked like that of an old woman's in a National Geographic photo, while the untouched breast was engorged to the size of a cantaloupe. The baby slept peacefully when I got up, so I didn't wake her to deflate my balloon-breast before leaving for my

8:00 a.m. thesis defense. I hoped the tan polyester suit jacket I'd bought on sale for the occasion covered the discrepancy in breast size.

I thought of her little face, how she looked as I left her that morning. Petite red eyebrows and eyelids moving as she pursed her lips in her sleep. Probably dreaming about Mommy's milk. But that little smile could also have been for her older sister.

Why did I experience a milk let-down each time I thought of my younger daughter, I wondered? It was as if our relationship was entirely about food, instead of *almost* entirely about food. It had been the same with our first daughter, and even as a four-year-old, she turned to her mom when she was hungry. It contrasted sharply with my relationship with my own mother, where food was a source of punishment. I'd get a beating if I didn't have supper ready when she got home, and she once pummeled my face with raw hamburger. To have food represent the warmth and comfort I could give my children constantly surprised me.

I thought back on my graduate student career, unable to believe that it might be finally coming to an end. I'd been attracted to the field of epidemiology while reading scientific articles for my master's degree in medical sociology. My husband, Martin, and I had come to the University of Washington, so he could begin his career as a computer science professor and I could pursue graduate studies. We'd arrived in Seattle in 1978 with one baby. Since then, I'd received As in all my classes, easily passed the challenging proficiency exams, designed and conducted an epidemiologic study, and this past year had produced a second baby. Now I hoped to be rewarded for my hard work.

Epidemiology is all about numbers. Numbers with a heart. It's the study of diseases in populations, and our labs are the world of people. Epidemiologists look at large groups of people; obtain data on demographic, health, and lifestyle variables; and investigate whether any of those predict the risk of developing disease—all numbers. But we care deeply about what the numbers represent—all heart. We want to find ways to prevent disease from occurring, to prevent suffering.

I had no business getting a PhD. Raised by a single mother in Irish-American working-class Boston, I was better prepared by my upbringing to be a domestic rather than an academic, to be a divorcee than a married mother of two. The first in my family to obtain a college degree, here I was reaching for the pinnacle of intellectual achievement. By marrying a computer science professor from an upper-middle-class background, I had sped up several rungs on the social class ladder. And now I was trying to go even further.

A steady hammering pulled me out of my reverie. Construction, I thought. Although the university was not wealthy, a steady flow of government research grants that year required frequent space adjustment. As the pounding continued, I realized the sound came from the conference room I'd just left. I crept over to it and put my ear to the door, sure that someone would fling it open. I'd fall into the room and the professors would assume I'd been listening through the door. To my surprise, my ear-on-door distinguished the sound as knocking from the inside. Gingerly, I turned the knob and slowly opened the door. Someone on the other side gave it a pull. I stumbled and just caught myself before falling flat on my face. The five faculty members clustered near the door, laughing.

"We were locked in," one said.

"We thought you'd make us stay here until we approved your dissertation," said another.

Without knowing if I'd passed or failed, I couldn't share in their glee. I hoped they hadn't been knocking for long, and that the trauma of their captivity wouldn't make them decide against me.

"Congratulations, Anne, you passed." My supervising professor smiled warmly as he told me the news.

"That's wonderful. Thank you so much."

Outwardly calm, inwardly doing jumping jacks, I shook hands with each of the professors. They said nice things about my research and thesis.

"What do you plan to do next?" asked the statistician.

"I guess I need to submit my thesis work for publication and then look for a job." Two of the professors leaned forward as I spoke. When I was anxious or unsure of myself—about 90 percent of the time—my quiet voice became almost inaudible.

"Well, there aren't too many jobs in Seattle, unless you're really good," said the older epidemiologist. His unspoken assertion was that I wasn't one of the "really good."

The room darkened, my joy at passing ruined. The problem was that I believed him. I silently agreed that I wasn't "really good." I didn't stop to remember that few men described female students or professors as "really good." Years later, I realize that some of the glass ceiling in academia is because of inherent sexism—male professors tend to see female academics as intellectually inferior, as helpers rather than as leaders. But some of the problem lies with how people, including scientists, see the worthiness of others' work and accomplishments. If a researcher speaks and acts with authority and confidence, others accept that. Women, especially young women in training, tend to speak tentatively and softly. I've seen many instances where a scientist repeatedly describes his or her own work as superior and important, while the audience nods enthusiastically. And I've seen the converse—the researcher who fails to sell himself or herself is seen as mediocre. While people outside of academics might think that science is such a fact-based field that brilliant results speak for themselves, the opposite is sadly true. There are probably thousands of important results that never get attention because the investigator didn't broadcast loudly and widely enough.

The committee members signed my PhD warrant. Such a strange term —the *warrant*—as if I'd be arrested for pretending to know something, pretending to be smart. How could my professors have been fooled? All but the one who was onto me, who saw my limitations. But even he signed the form. I was officially a Doctor of Philosophy.

"Congratulations, Dr. McTiernan," said my supervisor as he shook my hand again. I smiled broadly but wanted to look behind me for someone with my name who was the real doctor.

Bicycling home on Seattle's wooded Burke-Gilman Trail, I tried out my new title: Doctor McTiernan, Doctor Anne, Doctor, Doc. It felt unreal. I knew I wasn't a *real* doctor, not the medical kind who performs miracles, saves lives, and makes loads of money. But I could still use the title "Doctor." I might not be "really good," but I had the prestige of the PhD. I'd made it.

I pulled up to our little bungalow three miles northeast of the University of Washington. The house and its neighborhood clones had been built for GIs returning after WWII. Our home had three bedrooms, and we'd added a second bathroom. It was the first house I'd ever lived in. As a baby and toddler, I lived in day-care homes and institutions, and as a child, I lived with my mother and aunt in a series of rented flats in Boston. I loved our little Seattle home, although I looked forward to someday moving up in the world of Seattle real estate. "Moving up" in Seattle was often literal, such as living on top of a hill that provided a view of water or mountains, which could increase house prices by $100,000 or more.

I craned my head to look up at our house that was set above a rockery thick with overgrown golden alyssum, white candytuft, and blue lithodora. Horsetails stuck out of every free crevice, as if asserting the dominance they'd had for the past fifteen million years. A thick patch of St. John's Wort nestled against the front of the house. I hated that plant but at least it had color for some parts of the year. A six-foot-tall camellia bush grazed the bottom of the dining room window. Remnants of its glorious magenta blossoms littered the ground around it. I yearned for a gardener to clean up our yard, but we didn't have the funds, and my husband would never agree anyway. "It's not necessary," was his favorite three-word sentence. Our house had pale blue vinyl siding that we'd had installed after a botched paint job left the wooden siding blistered and peeling. We weren't too eco-conscious in those days, not realizing that the manufacture of vinyl siding required use of cancer-causing chemicals and that the siding could never be recycled.

I leaned my hot pink Schwinn bike against the rockery, knowing my husband would put it into the garage for me. His parents raised him to be chivalrous.

Inside the front door, the house smelled of last night's hamburgers mixed with dirty diaper. My four-year-old daughter greeted me with "Mommy, can you read me this book?" Rachel was tall for her age, her peaches-and-cream complexion framed by glorious wavy red hair. The glasses she'd begun wearing that year added to her cuteness, but I secretly lamented not being able to see her beautiful green eyes as clearly now.

Three-month-old Cassie wailed when she saw me, as if I'd been away for months. Her own peaches-and-cream skin reddened with her fury, contrasting with her wisps of tangerine hair. Her blue eyes held tears. She was all perfection, all motion. My husband leaned down to give me a quick congratulatory kiss and left to teach his class. I settled in to a normal afternoon with the girls: a sandwich for Rachel, mommy milk for the baby, a half hour preparation to walk the five minutes to the local park, home again after a half hour, snack for Rachel, library books on the couch, more mommy milk for the baby.

We had furnished our little house almost entirely with hand-me-downs and self-made items. Our maple wood dining room set and two Morris chairs had belonged to my stepfather's father. I'd scraped, sanded, and refinished the furniture on a college summer vacation in Massachusetts. A colonial print loveseat still bore stains of Cheetos left by the children of a graduate student who stayed with me in Buffalo when she fled her abusive husband. Our stereo set sat on boards Martin had purchased and stained for our first apartment in Toronto. I'd sewn chair cushions, slipcovers, curtains, and bedspreads. A perennially out-of-tune upright Baldwin piano completed our first-floor décor.

Martin and I had been married for six years. His parents were European Jews who had escaped the Holocaust. My mother had called his family "those people." As when she told me shortly after he and I started dating, "Those people only marry their own kind. Don't waste your time with him." Later she would come to like him more than she liked me, which wasn't saying much.

An only child, I'd always dreamed of a big family. Martin wanted two children. I had hoped for at least three but was reluctant to press Martin on this. I was not a woman of steel. I didn't know how to present my feelings, my wants, so I avoided conflicting topics. That meant I avoided many things. On a rare date night out, Martin would ask what movie I'd like to see. "I don't care," would always be my answer. So, I let Martin decide. Luckily his tastes leaned toward arty, romantic films, and he hated violence on the screen as much as I did.

Later in the afternoon, my first thought for dinner was the usual on my nights to cook: order pizza. My husband and I split a can of Miller Lite over dinner to celebrate my success. I watched him as he gobbled several slices. Tall and slender, he never put on weight despite eating copious amounts of food. With his coke-bottle bottom wire-rimmed glasses, bushy brown hair, t-shirt and worn jeans, he looked like a typical computer science professor.

As I lay in bed that night, I fretted about not being "really good" and about my poor chances of getting a job. While my husband made enough money to keep us fed and sheltered, we'd never be able to have some of the things I aspired to, like a Volvo station wagon, Starbucks coffee, Oshkosh clothing for my kids, and a water-view house in Laurelhurst. And because our four-year-old daughter had been reading since she was three years old, I aspired to private school for her. I needed money.

Chapter 2

APRIL 1983
TO FEBRUARY 1984

Ten months after my PhD defense, I landed a job. Well, not a real job. Officially, I would be a postdoctoral fellow, a "postdoc." I'd join the illustrious army of highly trained researchers working long hours for little pay, few benefits, and no guarantee of continued employment. In some institutions, people remain in postdoc positions for a decade or more after finishing their PhDs. They support the labs and make brilliant discoveries, but never attain the exalted position of Principal Investigator.

Still, I was excited to be employed and to be able to work in research. In my new position in the University of Washington School of Dentistry, I would investigate the prevalence of cavities. My PhD supervisor, upon learning that an epidemiologist was needed to help with research in the dental school, had referred me. I knew nothing about dentistry outside of my dreaded yearly checkup and the memory of many childhood fillings suffered without anesthetic. Coming from a poor family, with no funds for braces, my crooked lower teeth and upper overbite remained uncorrected. I hoped my new boss wouldn't be too put off by my dental deficits.

I began my fellowship in April 1983. The typical Seattle spring day—in the high forties and rainy—didn't dampen my excitement. Martin had the kids that morning, so I left early to bike into the office. I enjoyed the postage-stamp gardens of my neighborhood as I coasted down the slight incline toward the university. Spring arrives early in the Northwest. Crocuses had come and gone in January, followed by camellias in February. Cherry trees peaked in March. Now the rhododendrons were spectacular in my working-to-middle-class neighborhood. After a half mile, my route dropped me onto the Burke-Gilman Trail. Empty and green, it smelled faintly of cedar.

The dental school was located on the university's south campus. The medical complex abutted the easternmost section of the Lake Washington Ship Canal, which linked the lake to Puget Sound via Lake Union. The south campus was constructed of more than twenty wings built over more than fifty years, with the interior hallways fully connected. My PhD classes had been in the F wing, and my student carrel had been in a leaking, unheated, moldy annex that shook whenever someone opened the door. I'd now be working in the dental school's D wing offices.

If I'd taken the time, I could have meandered along one of the walkways that line either side of the canal. Years later, as a physician specializing in health promotion, I appreciate the need for exercise and nature to optimize one's health and well-being. But back then, if I wasn't working or studying, I was taking care of my children. I had no time to wander.

My little cubicle upstairs in the dental school had an old wooden desk, just big enough to read computer printouts without the reams falling over the back edge. But little work would be done in my office space. All programming had to be done at the south campus computing center. There, I'd type a program into a terminal and give instructions about what data tapes to load. Then I'd walk the half mile back to my office and wait until I thought my job should be done. Sometimes my program output would be all ready for me, looking fresh and crisp in the computer center's outbox. Other times, I'd have been wildly off in my estimate of job length and would have to decide whether to wait at the center, shifting from one foot to the other or trudge back to my office. I used data that the US government had collected as part of its ongoing study called the National Health and Nutrition Examination Survey, or NHANES. Between 1971 and 1974, NHANES dentists examined the teeth and gums of thousands of children and adults across the US. They counted the number of cavities and the number of teeth affected. They also examined the health of study participants' gums and recorded detailed information about the size of gum pockets—deeper indicates likely presence of infection and inflammation—around each tooth. I was tasked with studying associations of these data on teeth with some other variables that I cannot recall. I just remember the teeth.

My postdoc supervisor was a well-respected academic dentist. When he hired me, he told me that the funding for my salary came from a National Institutes of Health grant, which limited salary to $14,000 a year. Even in 1982 dollars, this was a poverty-level wage.

"But don't worry, I'll get supplemental funds from my department to raise your salary," he said.

"Okay," I said.

"But your husband is working, right?"

I nodded. "Yes, he's an assistant professor in the Computer Science department."

"So, you should be okay with whatever salary we come up with."

Stupidly, I nodded again. I never saw that supplemental salary.

The work turned out to be mildly interesting, except that dental researchers seemed to be more interested in teeth than in people.

Instead of counting the number of individuals with dental decay in a population, they counted the number of teeth with cavities. It would be like breast cancer researchers counting the number of affected breasts instead of the number of women with breast cancer. But I learned some things about a major public health problem and could work with some national data sets.

I met weekly with my supervisor in his cramped faculty office dominated by a bookshelf stuffed with texts like *Dental Anatomy*, *Physiology and Occlusion*, *Head and Neck Anatomy for Dentistry*, and *Oral Radiology*. It always struck me as odd that physicians learned so much about the entire human body but left out the mouth. Dentistry was completely separate from medicine.

During our meetings, I'd show him the results of data analyses and he'd talk at length about his academic career. He told me about his practice and the specialized clinic he wanted to establish. He talked about the grants he hoped to get and the papers he had written and presented at prestigious conferences. It was a perfect match—he liked to talk, and I didn't know what to say. It went along like this for about a month. I'd analyze more data, show it to him, and he'd say let's keep looking.

On the day that his hand strayed to my knee, I decided to look for another job. I couldn't concentrate on his words. I wanted to kick my leg up to dislodge his hand, hopefully mashing his balls in the process. I wanted to scream, "What the fuck do you think you're doing?" even though the "f" word felt so wrong that I never used it. But I said nothing, frozen by fear of confronting him. I worried he'd take offense and fire me on the spot. And maybe it was just innocent. My husband put his hand on our four-year-old daughter's knee. It could be a fatherly thing. I didn't have a dad in my life so had no experience with fatherly affection. That's it, I decided. It's just a fatherly thing. But if his hand strays up or down, I'm out of there. After suffering for what was probably just a few minutes but felt like an eternity, I quietly said that I had to leave to pick up my daughters. He moved his hand as if nothing untoward had happened, smiled, and said, "See you next week."

Biking home that day, my right knee felt the heat of the dentist's hand. Heat in a creepy way, not in a good sexual way or a reassuring parent-child way. I was a dedicated, loyal wife but I wasn't a nun. I found other men attractive. But the ones I was attracted to never touched me, not even a little pat on the arm or shoulder. Not a single hug hello. And the cute ones didn't even flirt with me. Either I was attracted to the aloof types, the ones who were not in touch with their feelings or, more likely, I liked the type of guy who respected the institution of marriage and did not proposition married women. It had been the same during my short dating stint between high school and marriage at age twenty-three. I didn't date men who were married or in relationships. In graduate school, I learned with horror that a current boyfriend had been having a secret affair with another classmate. At first, I couldn't understand why this woman threw nasty comments at me, until another friend explained the situation. So, was I the Other Woman or the Wronged Woman? Luckily, marriage saved me from dealing with this sort of situation again.

When I had envisioned my new scientific career, I didn't foresee a hand-on-knee moment, nor my reaction. My thoughts had run more to what interesting scientific discoveries I would make. Maybe I'd unearth some unknown causes of disease so that people could learn what to do to prevent this disease. I thought of the brilliant scientific manuscripts I would write. I'd publish the papers in top medical journals and my colleagues would notice and congratulate me.

The term "sexual harassment" hadn't yet made its way into our everyday speech. There was no #MeToo campaign. In the early 1980s, if a male boss made an advance or touched you inappropriately, you just dealt with it. Mentioning your husband sometimes helped—I noticed that many men seemed afraid of angering my spouse even if they didn't worry about offending me. Or you just sucked it up, hoping it would stop. Or you quit.

Looking back, I wonder if the lack of women in the dental school contributed to the professor's action. There were no female faculty members that I could see, although the support staff—secretaries and administrators—were primarily female. Perhaps it was just the culture at the time. I once noticed a faculty member give typing work to a secretary. His hand brushed against her breast as he leaned over. He apologized immediately, and she said no problem. But I wondered how a hand could accidently brush against a breast.

Maybe my dental professor, used to dealing exclusively with male colleagues, didn't know what to do with a female postdoc. Maybe he thought he should pet me, like "good doggie," when I performed well. Perhaps he thought the paycheck was a treat for being a good pet, because, with my husband's income, I didn't actually *need* my salary. I should have begged ("good doggie") for the salary supplement I'd been promised but never received.

The hand-on-knee could have had other meanings. The boss who puts his hand on his subordinate's shoulder is showing his superiority. It's a pecking order—the employee would not lay a hand on the boss. Or perhaps it mirrored the locker room slap-on-the-butt behavior? I'd never been in a male locker room so only knew of this from what I saw in movies.

Whatever the reason for the touch, it felt wrong and I didn't want to deal with it. It wasn't as if I wanted to dedicate my life to teeth. I was more interested in cancer research and women's health. So, I cut my losses, gave a two-week notice, and ran. My postdoc position of only two months' duration was probably one of the shortest on record at our university.

I didn't tell Martin about the hand-on-knee, afraid he'd tell me I was silly to worry about this. Perhaps he'd say I should just tell the professor not to do that again. My husband had no experience with being treated as less important because of his sex. He just worked hard, concentrated, proved brilliant theorems, published his scientific manuscripts, and taught new generations of computer scientists. His superiors and peers evaluated him on his results. They did not judge him on how he looked or on whether he acquiesced to a senior professor's intimate advances.

I told Martin I left the postdoc because the work was boring and not the type of epidemiology I'd been trained to do. Martin approved of this. A true academic, he understood the critical need to love your scientific area of work. If a problem doesn't excite a scientist, he (or she) won't have the motivation to pursue it to the end.

I was back to square one. I made appointments with a dozen epidemiology faculty members. The conversation went the same with each: I handed over my short resume, said I was looking for a position, and the professor said sorry he or she didn't have anything but would pass on my resume to others. Months passed. I began to despair of obtaining any job. My highest level of qualification was for analyzing data and writing up scientific reports, and, in Seattle at the time, few institutions needed people with such skills. I'd held jobs since I was thirteen years old but all had been service or clerical jobs. With the advent of computers, I'd finally learned to type. As a last resort, I could find a secretarial job, preferably one where the boss didn't put his hand anyplace on my body.

The last professor on my list was the member of my thesis committee who had hinted that I wasn't "really good." I met with him at his office in the Fred Hutchinson Cancer Research Center's main building on

Seattle's Pill Hill, so-called because of its density of hospitals and clinics. In the reception area of "the Hutch," as it is known, young men dressed in shirts, ties, and stethoscopes hurried past. Beepers buzzed, and phones rang. A bald patient shuffled by in pajamas and slippers, pushing his intravenous medication pole. Like many Seattle buildings erected in the 1970s, the structure was gray, small, and looked temporary. The professor's office was on the Public Health Sciences hall that housed about a half dozen faculty and a smaller number of administrators. The faculty members here were all men—the one female professor was relegated to a shoddy annex a block away.

A busy secretary with teased and frosted hair and bright pink nail polish told me in a raspy voice that the doctor would be available in a few minutes. With no place to sit, I stood nervously outside his office. After a few minutes, his door opened, and a young woman emerged, laughing. She rolled her eyes at the secretary.

The doctor looked surprised to see me, then said, "Oh, yes, Anne. Come in."

I told him I was looking for a job as an epidemiologist but didn't bother to hand over my resume because I was sure he wouldn't hire me.

"What are you hoping for in the future?" he asked.

"I'd like eventually to have a faculty position."

"Can you leave Seattle?"

"No, my husband is a professor in the University of Washington computer science department."

"Well, we don't hire faculty from our own PhD program. We did hire one this year, but that's only because he's really good."

There were those two words again.

"However, I do have a new grant funded, and I'll need someone to manage it for me. It's a study to look for causes of breast cancer in men."

"Wow, that sounds very interesting!"

We talked some more about the study and what he had proposed to the government's National Cancer Institute that induced them to give him a grant to do the study.

"Tell you what, why don't you give me a copy of your resume, and I'll have Jane here get you a copy of the study protocol. Then you can look it over and see what you think. In the meantime, I'll see if the other faculty members will approve the hire. Your title at the Center would be Staff Scientist but you'd function as a project manager for this study."

I felt completely taken aback, and very excited, by his ready offer. A week later, he called to formally offer me the job. The salary was double what I'd received at the dental school. I'd be doing what I loved—running a study on the causes of cancer, analyzing data, and writing scientific papers. I had made it.

Martin and I talked about the new job. We agreed we didn't want, and couldn't afford, full-time day care. So, we decided to split the childcare ourselves with some hours of day care in the middle. With some temerity, I asked my new boss if I could work an early shift from 6:00 a.m. to 2:00 p.m., and to my delight he said that would not be a problem. Our older daughter was now in full-day kindergarten, and we arranged half-day care for the baby, now seventeen months old. I began working at the cancer center in September 1983, a little over a year after obtaining my PhD.

While the knowledge I'd gained in my PhD program was useful, I had much to learn about managing a real study. Part of my job was to develop a questionnaire to obtain information from men with breast cancer and from a sample of men without breast cancer. All of the men would be interviewed by a professional interviewer and would answer questions about their occupations, use of medications, diet, and health habits. The interviewers tried out the questions on practice patients and reported back on what worked and what didn't. At first, most things didn't work.

Frustrated, I grew convinced that I couldn't do this job. To add to my stress, my boss questioned every decision I made. I felt like he didn't trust me, didn't think I was up to the job. In retrospect, I appreciate why he did this. Studies in which you are collecting health information and medical data from people can't be fixed after the fact—you have to get it right the first time. He was just being a careful researcher. But I soon realized I wanted more—I wanted to be the person in charge. Underneath that wish, I wanted my boss to tell me I was "really good," but, sadly, that wasn't going to happen.

Breast cancer is very rare in men. In order to enroll a large enough number of men to have a sufficient sample, my boss had enlisted ten other cancer centers around the country to participate in the study. Staff at those centers would identify men with breast cancer and a comparable sample of men without cancer. They would then interview the men using the questionnaire we developed. As project manager, I coordinated the work at the sites, including that at our institution. I developed the protocol and procedures manual, furnished the questionnaire, provided detailed training, and monitored progress. I was the contact person for the study, the one to call with problems. The staff at the participating centers knew much more than I about conducting a study of this type. I quickly realized that I was overwhelmed but was not willing to admit it to myself, my boss, or anyone else. I just soldiered through and, due to the excellent work of the staff and my boss, the study succeeded.

As a Staff Scientist, I was a member of the faculty. At twelve o'clock sharp, the faculty members, all male, trudged across the street to the hospital cafeteria. I suspected that the brown bag lunches they clutched were made by their good little wives. Wanting to be part of the faculty in-crowd, I decided to join the lunch bunch. I double-stepped to keep up with them as they raced to their usual table. My boss introduced me to everyone, and they smiled and said hello. Things went downhill quickly from there. They didn't consciously exclude me; but, they couldn't help it. They had to talk about sports. Having been raised by females and now with a husband who had no interest in sports, I was lost. I didn't know a Sonic from a Husky from a Seahawk. From my perspective, those teams all consisted of men who ran around in circles and made a lot of money. As the conversation droned on, I ate my lunch of two Red Delicious apples and a chunk of cheddar cheese. I tried to look interested. After a couple of weeks of this charade, I was miserable but didn't know how to extricate myself from the group lunches. For the first time in my life, I wanted out of the in-crowd.

One day as I left the cafeteria, I ran into two female statisticians who worked for my boss.

"How can you stand to sit there with them?" one of them asked.

"I can't. I'm going nuts."

"Have lunch with us instead."

"Oh, I would absolutely love that."

I was deeply grateful that these two women allowed me into their circle. They saved my sanity with their laughter, intelligence, and refusal to talk sports.

After I'd been working for several months, my boss hired a male staff scientist to manage a different study. This man had a PhD in a nonmedical field. So, in the hierarchy of epidemiologists, he was less qualified than I was.

Late one afternoon, a senior administrator for our department called me into her office. She closed the door and put her finger to her lips. Then she pointed to a piece of paper on her desk. I looked down and saw a list of names with numbers beside them. She pointed to my name and ran her finger along the row to the number, which I recognized as my yearly salary. Then she moved her finger up to another name—that of the new staff scientist. With a shock, I saw that his salary was 50 percent higher than mine. My mouth dropped open as I looked up at her. She still said nothing. I whispered a thank you and returned to my office.

As I sat shaking with rage, I realized that the administrator had taken a huge risk in revealing this information. Salaries were confidential at the cancer center. She could be fired for her action. In spite of the anger boiling up in me from my new knowledge, I felt grateful to this woman for helping me. She had no guarantee that I'd keep her complicity secret.

I had no idea how much money anyone else in our department made. Now I knew that a recent hire with fewer credentials was awarded a much higher salary. The following day, I broached the subject with my boss.

"I see you've hired the new staff scientist to help with one of your other studies."

"Yes, I've won too many grants to handle on my own. It's either a feast or a famine here."

"That's great. So, will he be functioning like I do?"

"Yes, he'll be managing my oral contraceptives and breast cancer study."

"Okay. Then he shouldn't be making 50 percent more money than I make."

"Oh, God," he groaned. He looked at me for a full minute. I stared back. Then he said, "I'll see what I can do."

To my surprise, he brought my case to the other faculty at their monthly meeting. They approved a 50 percent raise for me. Perhaps I was now "good enough."

Chapter 3

MARCH 1984

My job, with its spanking new salary, would be temporary. It would last only as long as the grant lasted—four years—which my boss had been honest about from the start. After the study ended, I'd have to find another researcher to hire me or hope that my boss kept me on for a new study. Staff scientists were let go for no reason other than that their bosses decided they were no longer a good fit. This was not a union job.

I also continued to be irritated at being questioned on every detail. I wanted to be the person in charge. Some PhD-trained epidemiologists in Seattle secured tenured faculty jobs at the University of Washington or the Fred Hutchinson Cancer Research Center to develop their own research programs. But there were few such opportunities, especially for a thirty-year-old woman.

The epidemiologists who were also physicians had less trouble landing academic jobs than the PhDs, and they earned a lot more money. In addition, many of them combined an academic career with seeing patients and teaching medical students, an intellectually and emotionally rewarding trifecta. From my interactions with the doctors in my epidemiology classes, it was clear that their knowledge of biology, disease, and medicine gave them a distinct advantage over those of us with just PhD training.

For most people, having a PhD would be plenty. However, I wanted more. I wanted to be at the top of the heap, to be the best of something.

Being a good mom was incredibly important to me. Not that I really knew what a good mother was. My own mother did whatever she could to get rid of me, as if I were an unwanted invader. Cancer doctors kill an invading tumor with several weapons—surgery, radiation, and chemotherapy—slash, burn, and poison. This attacks the invading tumor from many fronts, with the hope of eradicating it. My mother, in her quest to eradicate me, slashed me with her striking hand, burned me with her words, and poisoned me with her silence.

My mother discovered she was pregnant with me after five tumultuous years of marriage. My conception took place after her parish priest ordered her to return to her alcoholic, cheating husband with the admonition that God had joined her to this man forever. When she told my father that she was expecting, he erupted in a drunken rage, saying he didn't want her brat while throwing a chair at her. She kicked him out, thinking she'd rather risk God's wrath than my father's violence. My mother later informed me that had abortion been available at that time, she would have taken care of the "problem."

Her only sister moved in with my mother and stayed for fifteen years. My Aunt Margie served as a loving safety cushion between my mother and me.

My mother told me that with only twenty dollars per week court-required child support from my father (which he rarely paid), she had to choose between welfare and working. She chose to work. She discovered that my crying at night bothered her sleep. When adding cereal to my milk bottle didn't work, she decided to send me to live in child-care homes during the week. At three months of age, I began my five years of living in homes and institutions; I'd come home only on weekends. In the first one, the owner—a woman called Honey—fed the toddlers dinner while they sat on potty chairs. Multitasking, I guess. My doctor told my mother to take me out of that home after he saw the dangerous infection I'd contracted from unchanged diapers. A loving nurse ran my second care home. Her charges were children too sick for their parents to be able to care for them. I was the only healthy child in her charge. This home, unfortunately, had to relocate to another state because of licensing regulations. I remember my last institution vividly: at age four, I moved into a Catholic boarding school where I lived for most of a year and almost starved to death.

All my life, I yearned for an intact family—mother, father, children. Denied this as a child, I was determined to have it as an adult. I chose a man who had been raised with a strong family-focused ethic. He had seemed like he would be a good father, and he never disappointed. I didn't want my children to experience what I had endured. Martin and I would provide a stable home for them. I would never send them away. Neither Martin nor I ever hit our girls. I rarely raised my voice. But I stumbled through motherhood. From other moms, I learned that babies are calmed by being walked outdoors in a carrier or stroller, that toddlers love to be read to, that play dates were a thing, that educational toys were better than commercial toys. These were easy skills to mimic. But I felt that these mothers were more nurturing than I could ever hope to be. The fact that my girls were developing normally and beautifully didn't reassure me at all.

There was no way to remedy my feelings of inadequacy other than facilitating more Dad time and making sure the girls had access to other adults who could give them additional loving care. Looking back, I want to shake myself. If I was so insecure as a mom, why didn't I do something constructive like read books on parenting or seek counseling?

It never occurred to me to go to a therapist—in the working-class world I'd grown up in, shrinks were for psychotic people. I feared that if I ever let a professional know what went on in my head, he'd lock me up in an insane asylum. And I assumed that if Martin knew I had to see a shrink, he'd leave me and take the kids with him.

So I thought if I could excel in my work life, I could compensate for my other inadequacies.

I'll become a doctor, I decided. I'll be rich and important.

I hoped that by becoming a doctor I'd finally be okay. I'd be respected, admired. I wanted this so badly that I asked my family to make significant sacrifices for me without any guarantee that they would benefit. Sure, I'd bring more money into the family as a doctor, but it would be at least four years before I could make big bucks as a physician researcher. Martin wasn't particularly interested in having more money— his solution to financial balance was to keep spending to a minimum rather than trying to make more. (He should have been a professional financial advisor.) And the girls stood to gain very little from my becoming a doctor. They didn't care what job their mommy had, as long as she was at home to comfort their boo-boos, make snacks, and find their lost shoes and dollies. They had no concept of money—they either had things or not but didn't seem particularly bothered by a limited budget.

I fretted about how to broach my scheme with Martin. I couldn't do this on a whim. While I hoped to be able to attend the University of Washington School of Medicine, I had to face the fact that it might not admit me. Spots in medical schools, especially high-ranked ones such as the University of Washington, were extremely competitive. I had several strikes against me. I was not the typical applicant at the time—male, twenty-two years old, single, without responsibilities. I was female, thirty years old, married, and a mother of two young children. Most doctors came from professional families, often with physician dads. I grew up in poverty, raised by a secretary.

I'd have to apply to schools around the country, since the University of Washington was the only medical school in our state. If it didn't accept me, the move to another state would be a major upheaval in the lives of my husband and children. Martin would give up a tenured faculty position. The girls would be pulled from their friends, schools, activities, and everything they knew, and transplanted to new schools where they would have the trauma of meeting and making new friends. There would be a financial burden. The four years' tuition would cost as much as $100,000—and I wouldn't bring in a salary during that time. While I could get a loan, and my high physician salary later would more than make up for these expenses, we'd take a short-term financial hit. The clinical years in the second half of medical school with their required on-call duty would be a challenge.

I'd heard of husbands who'd opposed their wives going to medical or other professional schools, especially if there were children involved. I assumed Martin would be one of those. I broached the subject one evening after the girls were in bed and quiet, and before he'd settled in to prepare his next day's lecture. I sat kitty-corner to him at our warped maple-wood dining room table, so I could put my hand on his. I wrapped my other hand around my mug of tea, hoping the warmth would sooth me.

"I've been thinking I'd like to go to medical school."

"Really? Why? That sounds crazy." His eyes were wide. His free hand twirled a pen.

"Well, my job isn't secure at all, and there's no possibility of my getting a faculty position without having the MD degree." Martin understood this part. His department never hired their own graduates into faculty slots—something about making sure the department retained diverse sources of training and knowledge. (Of course, that diversity policy didn't extend to hiring many women or minorities back in the '80s.)

"What would it involve?" he asked.

"Well, I'd have to take the MCAT."

"What's that?"

"The Medical College Admission Test. It's a full day of multiple-choice questions. Like the GRE, only it's focused on biology and chemistry." He understood this, too. Every prospective graduate student took the Graduate Record Exam before applying for master's or PhD programs.

"Then I'd need to apply to medical schools around the country."

"What about the University of Washington medical school? I'm sure they'd take you."

"That would certainly be my top choice. But there's no guarantee they'd accept me. It all depends on my MCAT scores and my grades."

"But your grades were great."

"My graduate school grades were good. It's the undergraduate science classes they look at. And there's no hiding the C-minus that I got in the second semester of college chemistry after my bike accident."

Martin sat quietly for a minute. I waited, barely breathing. He leaned back in his chair.

"I'd have to give up my tenured position if we moved to a new city."

"Would you be able to get it back when we return?"

"I don't know. I'll have to talk to the department chairman," he said.

He said nothing for a minute. I felt tears starting to form, knowing now that he wouldn't agree to move.

"Will it make you happy?" he asked.

"Yes, if I get in."

"Then let's do it."

"Thank you," I said quietly.

꩜

Martin's and my backgrounds couldn't have been more different. No one in my family had attended college. For most of my childhood, I lived with my mother and Aunt Margie. I didn't meet my father until I was sixteen years old. My relatives were always angry at each other, and my concept of family was something tenuous, easily broken with a cross word.

Martin's parents met in New York, married, and moved to a commuters' town in New Jersey. Martin's dad had a college degree and was an actuary and vice president of a New York insurance company. His mom worked part-time as a bookkeeper. His maternal grandmother, who spent four years in a Japanese prisoner-of-war camp after she and her husband traveled the globe to flee the Holocaust, lived with them. Martin's concept of family was something safe, sheltering, never to be shattered.

Martin and I were similar in several ways, however. We were both intelligent and academic. Our favorite pastime was reading, although since becoming parents, we got our plot fixes from children's books rather than novels of our own choosing. We weren't particularly athletic, although we enjoyed walking in nature. Our children were our priority, and we agreed on most childrearing issues. We taught the girls the right and wrong ways to behave and never used physical means of discipline. We didn't give the girls a religious upbringing. I was still reeling from the shackles of my Catholic childhood and didn't want my girls to endure that. I also couldn't let go of fearing other religions, drummed into me in my Catholic youth; part of me worried that I'd go to hell if I joined another religion. Martin didn't believe in any faith.

But we differed in our need for expressions of affection. I desperately wanted to be loved, to hear Martin say the words. When I asked him if he loved me, he'd say, "I have trouble expressing emotions." I assumed that his problem with saying the words meant that he didn't have the feeling. Because of this, I worried that he'd leave me. That was my childhood experience—men don't stay with women. So, hearing him say that he'd be willing to move in order to make me happy was comforting. Even if he didn't love me, he was at least committed to me.

One rainy evening, we attended a computer science department potluck party for Martin's faculty, graduate students, and families. University funds were tight in those days, so we all crammed into the basement of a professor's house and drank cheap keg beer. The faculty wives stood near the food table laden with guacamole, chips, and three-bean salads. The professors (all male) stood in groups of two or three, sipping beer from red plastic cups. The graduate students, mostly male, crammed into a far room where a boom box blared heavy metal. I held the squirming two-year-old Cassie in my arms to keep her out of trouble, while keeping an eye on the bored six-year-old Rachel and talking with a couple of other moms. After a while, I realized it was getting late. Dragging the girls, I went to look for Martin, whom I found in the far room dancing with a young woman who had her eyes closed. I stood and stared at him, but he didn't look at me. The song ended. Martin and the young woman exchanged words I couldn't hear. He walked over to me and said it was time to go. Later, after the girls were in bed, I asked him who he was dancing with, and why he danced with her when he never would dance with his own wife? He replied that the student asked him.

I had so many questions. *Did he find this young woman so much more attractive than me that he'd dance with her when she asked, when he wouldn't ever dance with me? And who was this woman, asking a married professor to dance with her? Was she a home wrecker? Did she have a crush on my husband? Was he having an affair with her? Would he leave me for her?* I didn't tell him the pain this caused me, afraid to let him know that I felt old, fat, ugly, and unlovable, and worried that he'd leave me for a new, young woman. I didn't want to anger him. I knew that he would leave me if I made him angry. Because that's what men do. Because that's what my father did. So I held my feelings in and hid the pain— but I couldn't hide the pain from myself.

If I get accepted to medical school everything will be all right, I told myself. Then I'll feel important and okay about myself and won't worry about Martin leaving me.

Chapter 4

Free to move ahead, I embarked on a course of action. I had already taken the prerequisite science courses (biology, chemistry, organic chemistry, physics, calculus) in college and graduate school. I studied for the MCAT and answered thousands of practice questions but didn't have the time or money to take a preparation course. I learned later that most premed students (or more accurately, their parents) shelled out big bucks for the prep courses to inflate their test scores.

I took the MCAT exam in the spring of 1984—a grueling half day of filling in circles with Number 2 pencils in a sterile gray room with stern patrolling proctors. If my scores on that exam fell below a certain cutoff point, I could forget about going to medical school. I scored very high on the aptitude sections but not so high on the science knowledge sections. I prayed my graduate school work and aptitude scores would impress the admissions officers enough that they would overlook my gaps in knowledge about biology.

Martin and I drew up a list of cities with computer science research facilities and medical schools. We came up with six—Seattle, New York, Boston, Pittsburgh, Atlanta, and San Francisco. He would apply for both faculty and research positions in these cities. Most of the cities had more than one medical school, which would increase my chances. Seattle, unfortunately, had just the one.

In the midst of this planning, I turned to a doctor who had taken epidemiology classes with me. Sam was a professor in the University of Washington School of Medicine. He took care of patients, taught medical students, conducted research, and was quick with a joke and a smile. I figured he'd have some good advice for me as I endeavored to morph from epidemiologist to "real" doctor. He agreed to meet with me at Harborview, Seattle's inner-city hospital, before his afternoon clinic.

As I waited in the hospital's cafeteria, the smell of hamburgers warming under heat lamps made me slightly nauseous as it dredged up memories of institutional food from my childhood. To distract myself, I watched the tall, handsome doctors stride by in their long white coats. They resembled the white-robed gods of antiquity, holders of sacred knowledge and power over life and death. They wore pagers on their belts, stethoscopes around their necks, and pens stuffed into their pockets. This paraphernalia made them look even more important. I so badly wanted to join their ranks.

My friend rushed in, looking a little harried.

"What can I help you with?" he asked after we'd grabbed some lunch.

"I'm applying to medical school and wondered if you had any advice for me." As usual, I hadn't prepared specific questions. I must have hoped he'd guess what I wanted to know.

"Ooh, that's tough. You have kids, right?"

"Yes, two girls."

"How old are they?"

"Our older daughter is six, and the little one is two years old."

"That's going to be hard."

"Why?"

"Med school is brutal. It'll be murder on your family."

I waited for him to go on.

"I'd advise you not to do it."

I was disappointed. I'd wanted him to tell me how wonderful it was to be a doctor and to reassure me that I'd get accepted somewhere. I'd wanted him to say I'd make a great doctor and that I'd have a perfect life. Silently, I attributed his warnings to sexism. He'd never have said those things to a man, I thought.

"Well, I hope I helped," he said. I smiled and thanked him for his time.

Zipping north on the I-5 freeway, back in the '80s before Seattle had traffic problems, I mulled over his words. Sam didn't know my family. He didn't realize how capable a parent Martin was. He didn't understand how badly I needed to become a doctor. I decided to stop asking people for advice.

Not much of a risk-taker, I was surprisingly calm about this gamble. The one time I rode on a rollercoaster, clutching Martin for dear life, I vowed never to do it again. On our honeymoon, I hiked up a mountain in the Alps rather than take the aerial lift because I feared that the metal box dangling from one skinny wire would smash to tiny pieces with me inside. I refused to do many other things: ride a horse, skydive, fly in a small plane, scuba dive, and ride a bicycle down a steep hill. I couldn't handle any more stress than what my rather ordinary life provided. Some people have bucket lists of things they wanted to do. I had buckets of things to avoid. I'd had enough terror in my life, being abused in many different homes and institutions. Now my terrors were from things like being called on in class, thinking Martin would leave me if I expressed any anger, and watching my girls play on the monkey bars.

My uncharacteristic calm approach to applying to medical school was fueled by brash determination. I knew that by becoming a physician, I'd become a different, better person.

I had limited experiences with medical professionals. Until graduate school, my contacts with doctors had been at the receiving end of a stethoscope, speculum, or scalpel. My childhood family doctor had saved my life by forcing my mother to remove me from the Catholic boarding school when I was five years old. He later performed some surgical procedures that would be questioned nowadays but were considered good medicine then. At age six, our doctor put me under full anesthesia to remove a smallpox scab that wouldn't heal. At age eight, I had a tonsillectomy, the most common surgical procedure in the US at the time. My gynecologist gave me oral contraceptives for menstrual cramps only after he first performed a uterine dilation and curettage that required an overnight hospital stay.

I viewed these physicians just as I saw the men of the Catholic Church—as all-knowing agents of God. They had the power of life and death over us mere humans. As a child, I saw no possibility of becoming one of these special persons. First, all of the doctors I'd met were men. I thought that nursing was the only medical profession open to women. Only after receiving a recommendation from a graduate school classmate did I visit a female gynecologist and discover that women really can be doctors. That gynecologist was a wife and mother. She was nothing like the men who'd treated me before. She suggested courses of action rather than directing me. She told me the scientific reasons behind her recommendations. And she seemed to love her job.

My second type of experience with doctors occurred in the University of Washington epidemiology program, where half of my classmates were physicians. Sitting next to them every day, struggling with the same material, had helped me see them as people first, doctors second. The fact that I earned better grades than some was helpful, although those with lower grades said it was because they were too busy with patients to be able to study. I didn't counter that, as a mom to two young children I also had little time for schoolwork.

So, while the young Anne would not have dared think herself worthy of becoming a doctor, the mature thirty-year-old Anne saw that she at least had the right to think about this career.

I asked two of my professors for letters of recommendation for medical school. Both were physicians. One, my thesis advisor, wrote in his letter that I was "more than adequate." His many students would know that he considered this phrase to be a compliment. Worried that the medical schools would interpret it to mean that I was a mediocre student, I begged him to revise it (he did, reluctantly). The other, my boss, wrote a glowing letter. I guessed his micromanagement of me was just his style, rather than his lack of faith in my ability.

That summer, I mailed applications to medical schools in our chosen six cities, and Martin and I awaited my University of Washington admission letter.

It didn't happen. Oh, I did have an interview at the University of Washington, early in the fall. For thirty minutes, three doctors lobbed questions so fast I wanted to duck.

Why did I want to go to medical school when I already had a PhD and a job?

I stuttered something about wanting to know medicine in order to be a better public health researcher. I didn't know how to say that, as a young woman, I felt like I needed extra credentials to compete for a tenure-track faculty job and to command a good salary.

Why should they give a spot to me rather than a young person who had better science grades than I?

I assumed they meant a young man. And how dare I ask to take the place of a man who really deserved to become a doctor. I shrugged my answer.

Where did you grow up?

In Boston.

That's a great city. You must have enjoyed growing up there.

Hmmm, people who think Boston is a great city are often upper class, intellectuals, elites. How to put my impoverished background into an appropriate answer for a medical school interview? I just said, "Yes."

Who was my childhood hero?

I couldn't answer without talking about religion. We Irish-Catholic kids were taught that our heroes, all men, were Jesus, the Apostles, the Jesuit missionaries who "saved" the New World, the Pope, and President John F. Kennedy, pretty much in that order. We had no choice of heroes. I said quietly that I didn't remember having a hero.

Why kind of books did I read?

Mostly mystery novels.

Why did I read mystery novels rather than books about human relationships?

How could I explain that I so adored books about relationships that if I was in the middle of one I would read until three or four in the morning to find out what would happen to the protagonist? This practice was barely sustainable when I was younger, but impossible after I had children. I didn't dare talk about motherhood, a liability in medical school admissions. So, I just said I liked them.

The interviewers must have thought I was a cold fish. They placed me on a waiting list, which gave me about a 5 percent chance of being accepted. With odds too long to rely on a University of Washington acceptance, we realized we'd most likely have to move.

Over the fall of 1984, I interviewed at several other medical schools. At Harvard, I arrived at a waiting area surrounded by male applicants, all ten years younger than I and towering at least a foot over my five feet four inches. They all looked smarter and more self-assured than I did. Nevertheless, I loved touring the historic lecture halls and imagined the famous physicians teaching there over the centuries. Alas, I wasn't Harvard medical school material.

New York University arranged for a professor to interview me when he visited Seattle for a meeting. He suggested we meet in a bar. Surprised, I agreed. He drank a beer. I sipped Diet Coke. For several minutes, he questioned me on why I wrote my application essay about meeting my father for the first time when I was sixteen years old. It was a strange thing to write, he said. His statements got me so rattled that I flubbed the rest of the interview. His medical school put me on a waiting list.

On a dark and snowy day in mid-December I had my interview at the University of Pittsburgh medical school. We traveled as a family; Martin would watch the girls while I met with a professor of pediatrics. Later, I'd take care of the girls while Martin interviewed at Carnegie Mellon's computer science department. I hoped my interview would not be too harsh—I still reeled from the University of Washington experience. I needn't have worried. The physician, a pediatrician, was warm and inviting. He asked particularly about my admissions essay.

"You had no dad in your life growing up?" he asked.

"No, my mother didn't remarry until I was seventeen."

"This is incredible. You've done so well in life, finished not only college but your PhD, married, and had children."

I smiled, not knowing what to say. Talking about my early family life was new to me. The medical school essay was the first time I'd put the story to paper, and I'd told few people other than my husband about my childhood.

"I just think you're an amazing survivor."

I wanted to hug this generous man. University of Pittsburgh Medical School accepted me, and I've always felt so grateful to my interviewer and to that school. Unfortunately, Martin didn't get a job offer in Pittsburgh.

After Pittsburgh, we traveled farther east. New York Medical College interviewed me on their beautiful campus in Valhalla, about thirty miles north of New York City. My evaluator, an oncologist, acted quite casual, almost dismissive. I assumed this meant he didn't want to waste time on a loser. Martin interviewed at IBM's prestigious Yorktown Heights research lab fifteen miles north of Valhalla. The girls visited their grandma—Martin's mom—in New Jersey while we had our interviews.

We had interviews at Emory in Atlanta for me, and at Georgia Tech for Martin. Martin recalls that both offered us positions.

New York Medical College accepted me before spring. IBM Research offered Martin a position. We accepted both.

I felt ecstatic. I was on my way to fame and fortune.

Our daughters were not so overjoyed. Rachel, now in second grade, understood that she would have to leave her friends. She'd leave the lovely girls who frequently spent afternoons at our house and sometimes slept over. She almost believed us when we said we'd come back to Seattle for visits. Cassie, a bouncy two-and-a-half-year-old, said she didn't want to go and wanted to visit her friends, too. I would also miss their friends, would miss the musical sound of girl giggling, the whispered planning for the next activity, but mostly the joy they brought to my daughters.

Martin spread a map of Westchester County, New York, on our dining table. We measured the distance from New York Medical College in Valhalla to IBM Research in Yorktown Heights and found the midpoint between the two—Chappaqua. That's where we'd live, we decided. IBM flew the four of us out to New York to shop for houses. This was an ego boost—I felt very corporate-fancy, getting a free trip to house-hunt. My previous moves had involved multiple trips with an overflowing trunk, graduating to a rented U-Haul that we'd pizza-bribe friends to help us load and unload.

In New York, we met with a real estate agent recommended by Martin's new employer. We told her where we wanted to live. She asked rather pointed questions about our salary, other sources of income, and our current house value. A little nosy, I thought. Then she told us what houses in our dream town would cost. We asked about the next town north—Millwood. She shook her head. She got out a map and we kept pointing to more little towns, moving north. She kept shaking her head. Finally, when Martin's finger landed on Yorktown Heights, eighteen miles north of Valhalla, she smiled. We could afford Yorktown Heights. We bought a split-level ranch on an acre of wooded land. Rachel would go to the excellent public school. Cassie would attend a Montessori preschool.

We put our Seattle house up for sale, and it sold within a week. Over the summer, we would fly east, visit family, and move into our new home.

On moving day, after all boxes and furniture were stored on the van that would take them 3,000 miles to our new home, I walked through the empty house. I recalled the happy times: the day Martin and I moved in with our baby daughter, Rachel, then just five months old. She sat on her own for the first time that day, comfortable on the living room's light brown plush carpet. I remembered the day we brought our second daughter home from the hospital; Martin and Rachel took much better care of us than the harried nurses had. The sounds of my children's laughter in that house were imprinted on my brain; I didn't need modern recording technology to remember them. It was a good house, a wonderful home for our family, but I was ready for the change. Like this bare house, my life was now a clean slate, ready for the move to New York and my new career.

Chapter 5

AUGUST 1985

Westchester County, New York

In early August 1985, we moved into the new house, unpacked, and found Cassie's "stuffed Sealie" that she'd asked about every day for the entire summer. Then we did critical moving-in things like picking up groceries and shopping for school clothes, backpacks, and lunch boxes for the girls.

Our new home on French Hill Road in Yorktown Heights sat on a small hill. A long driveway passed through a wooded area, skirted a neatly mown lawn, and led to the attached two-car garage at the side of the house. A walkway led around the house to the front door. The front door opened into a small foyer with a coat closet. The stairs to the right led down to the family room, laundry, and what once was a bathroom but was now the previous owners' darkroom. The stairs to the left led straight to our kitchen, living room, and dining area. From the top of these stairs, an Italian-tiled hallway led to three bedrooms and two bathrooms. The color scheme leaned heavily on olive and dark green. The kitchen wallpaper was particularly nauseating. Against a white background, orange, yellow, and olive-green squares marched within larger olive-green squares. It would irritate me for the four years we lived there.

I had convinced Martin to discard some of our low-end Seattle furniture. I now had my first opportunity to buy brand new furniture. We chose a tapestry-upholstered sectional couch that was large enough to hold two reclining adults and two squirming little girls. We also purchased a massive oak dining room table, six chairs, and hutch with glass doors. The salesman practically clapped with glee as Martin wrote out a check.

The back deck looked out on a wooded hill thick with maple, oak, and birch trees, the kind that produce psychedelic colors in the fall. Plenty of interspersed evergreen trees ensured our property would still be private in the winter. The sloping front lawn was too large for Martin's push mower to handle. Ornamental bushes and annual color plants lined the front of the house. The wooded area the driveway passed turned out to be a ravine. We immediately staked out verbal boundaries for the girls. In other words, we walked around with them and said, "Don't go there," while pointing to woods, the ravine, the underside of the back porch, and some shiny three-leaved plants that we suspected could be poison ivy.

In all, I liked the house. Its wooded property was spectacular, and because it hid us from view of the neighbors, it felt like a private retreat. I would come to appreciate that zen-like feeling more and more as the year progressed, until the woods could no longer calm me.

In our first week in the house, we moved quickly through rooms, up and down stairs, unpacking and getting organized. Three-year-old Cassie called, "Where are you, Mommy?" whenever she couldn't see me. I felt the same—adrift, not knowing where I stood in relation to my new world. Yet, I was thankful to have a home in a new town, hopeful for the girls' comfort and success in school, and excited about my coming adventures in medicine.

Medical school orientation began the last week of August. On the first day, I overshot the entrance to the medical school after driving the eighteen miles down the Taconic Parkway and connecting to the Sprain Brook Parkway. Looking for a place to turn around, I saw brick buildings similar to those of the college, but all were behind two rows of barbed-wire fencing. This fencing went on and on, until finally a small red sign with "New York Medical College" in gold lettering appeared with an arrow pointing left. I'd learn later that day that the Westchester County Correctional Center—a jail—shared the same campus as the medical school. It seemed ominous.

Located thirteen miles north of Manhattan, New York Medical College sat on a lush fifty-four-acre campus in Valhalla. In addition to the prison, it shared its campus with the Westchester County Medical Center, one of several hospitals that the medical students rotated through for clinical experience.

All day Monday, we sat in a large, dingy lecture hall and listened as administrators and important doctors told us how great we were. We were the selected ones, the chosen few. I felt great. (The following week, the PhD lecturers would wear down our egos, telling us just how little we knew. My mood would plummet to its usual low level.)

The director of financial aid talked for a long time about various aid packages, loans, grants, and scholarships. The students listened intently. I let my mind wander. Martin and I already had our aid package. Martin's mother had agreed to loan us the entire cost of my medical schooling, which would be about $100,000 over the four years. We signed an agreement to pay her back with 5 percent interest—lower than the banking rate at the time. I was grateful for her generosity. I had asked my aunt for the loan, but she said all her funds were tied up in her retirement account. I knew my mother didn't want to part with any money for me. And my father hadn't even paid child support as I grew up—he'd never agree to help. Martin and I had read over the medical school financial loan materials a few months prior. The application required that my parents supply a copy of their current tax returns, to prove that they couldn't pay for my education. I didn't want to hear the "no" from my mother or father, either to supplying tax returns or to an actual loan. We decided to approach Martin's mother. Many years later, after her death, we'd learn that she had given large sums of money to many relatives.

We finished the day with a plenary session to provide us with practical information, like the location and hours of student health, parking stickers, and student aid. Then a bearded young man stood up at the lectern. He wore a corduroy jacket with suede elbow patches.

"I'm Doctor Jones," he said. "I'm a psychiatrist here at the school. I'm also the student mental health liaison."

The room was silent.

"I'm going to write my phone number on the blackboard. When you need me, and many of you will, call this number."

He wrote the number in white chalk in three-foot high digits. Looking around, I saw students diligently copying the number into their notebooks. I wrote it down also, knowing I'd never call. In my Irish-Catholic tribe, psychiatrists were for deranged people. If I was insane, I didn't want to know it and didn't want anyone else to know either.

The following day began a series of orientations to our classes. I received my class schedule, the same as everyone else's. All 200 of us would be in the same large lecture hall, five days a week, from 9:00 a.m. to noon. The afternoons would be a mix of labs and physical exam skills. I would be able to take care of the girls a couple of afternoons a week.

This was also the day for purchasing supplies at the college's bookstore: textbooks (Clemente's *Anatomy*, Bates' *A Guide to Physical Examination*, and histology and cell biology textbooks), a pristine white lab coat, a stethoscope, a penlight, and index cards. I heard someone in line say that the cards were necessary for memorizing and for taking notes for patient presentations.

Wednesday was special for two reasons. Cassie's preschool teacher would come to our house at 8:30 a.m. to meet the family, and my anatomy lab orientation began at the same time. I'd have to miss meeting the teacher, the first of many family events I'd miss due to medicine and a constant source of tension. But Martin said he'd handle it, no worries. Cassie was less forgiving, and I had to gently extricate myself from the arms she wound tight around my legs. My excitement at starting medical school was reduced by her not wanting me to leave. I didn't want to leave her or her sister, either.

In my beige Volvo station wagon, I sped twenty minutes down the Taconic Parkway, built for half the number of cars going half the speed of its typical commuters. I arrived at the school late, hot, and breathless. I raced through halls to find my assigned anatomy lab section. Finally, I found the room, opened the door, and entered hell.

The anatomy professor raised one eyebrow at me as I slinked in, seemingly the last to arrive. On my way in, I had managed to get only one arm into my lab coat. I skirted the bodies, terrified of touching them. I wondered why the seats were one short—as if the professors were playing musical chairs and the one left standing would be "out." I was the odd one out at this medical school, where two-thirds of the students were male, most had medical genes passed down from their doctor-fathers and nurse-mothers, the average age was twenty-two, and all spoke the mile-a-minute New York vernacular.

Dead bodies surrounded me. Covered in white plastic, they lay supine. The odor of formaldehyde permeated the air and would sink into my clothes, hair, and skin for the remainder of the year. That smell would remind me day and night of the nearness of death. It stung my eyes; blinking didn't help.

"It goes without saying that you will treat your bodies with respect," the professor said. I figured she wasn't talking about our own bodies like the nuns lectured us in high school. No, she meant these dead people. She had a slight European accent, not Austrian or Hungarian like my in-laws. I read the name on her lapel—van Dorn—and thought she must be Dutch. Her skin and hair were as white as her lab coat. I couldn't estimate her height, since she sat, but imagined her as Viking-sized, ruler of the anatomy lab, holder of my future status as doctor or failure.

"You must remember that the corpses in the anatomy lab were once human beings. They have given a precious gift to you, young doctors, in letting you learn from their bodies. You must appreciate that always. You will not give your bodies names; you will not joke about them or make fun of them. And you will only perform the prescribed dissections, no others. Do you understand?"

Bug-eyed, we all nodded.

"We will begin with learning every muscle of the body," she said, "from the smallest to the largest. Can anyone tell me what is the smallest muscle in the body?"

Less than a split second elapsed before a male student spit out an answer: "The arrector pili."

"Yes, excellent," replied our Viking. "Where is this located?"

"In the hair follicle," the same student replied, not bothering to hide his smugness.

"Very good."

So, this was how it was going to be, I thought. While our professor talked on about the class structure, dissection, and written and practical exams, all I could think about was how I didn't even know there were muscles inside my hair follicles, much less their obscure name. I was a failure already.

I finished putting on my coat and hugged it closed. It fit my hips snugly, an annoying reminder of my Irish peasant build—small on top, big on bottom. My coat pockets held the index cards, still encased in a plastic wrapper. Later, I'd fill them with notes, wishing that I could slot these into my brain to help me memorize the thousands of anatomical names, positions, and functions.

That I'd been late to class I ascribed to my being a mom, having mom things to do at home. But maybe I arrived late out of fear. Who was I, pretending to be doctor material? I'd worshipped every doctor I ever met, in awe of their brilliance and power over life and death. I'd delayed applying to medical school because of the worry that I wasn't admission-worthy, not good enough to join this exclusive club. Now here I was, an imposter, mistakenly allowed into medical school. The dozen or so schools that had rejected me were right—I could never be a physician. The three or four schools that had accepted me had been fooled.

I worried about today's tardiness now. What if I'd missed some critical information that would be on the first exam? Would I get in trouble for not knowing what to do with these bodies that we were swimming amongst?

I glanced at the rest of the class as they listened intently. They all looked to be in their early twenties—barely over drinking age. The female students had big hair, padded shoulders, loud makeup, and polished nails. I couldn't see but knew they'd all have small hips squeezed into their tight designer jeans. I hated their tiny hips and envied their mascara and manicures. I'd barely found time to brush my hair and throw on clean clothes that morning before getting the girls ready. A manicure would have lasted less than one day even if I'd had time to have one, chips of polish mixing in with the raw veggies I cut up for our daughters each night because they refused to eat cooked vegetables. The male students looked self-assured, like future neurosurgeons.

We learned there would be five sections of our Gross Anatomy lab, each with forty students. "Gross" was a very apt term, I decided, concentrating again on that horrific smell that I wanted to escape. We would attend dissection lab three times a week.

The professor pointed to a bulletin board on which she had posted a list of our names along with a table number. Four students would be assigned to each table, meaning four to each body. "Table" in this case meant a steel gurney with a dead body lying atop it. We would take turns dissecting our assigned body. We would be graded on the neatness of our dissection, so we were responsible for the group's work as well as for our own. I had no idea what this meant. Should I wrest the scalpel from my tablemate's hand if he did a messy job? I pictured blood.

She introduced a junior teacher and a laboratory assistant; both would be available to help with our dissections. I wondered what would lead someone to a job like this. I hoped they received hazard pay.

Suddenly, the formerly white room looked gray and blurry. Or was it reddish like the inside of my eyelids? I felt dizzy and nauseous. My mouth and hands were numb. I wanted to sit down, but there still was no seat available. I realized this was how I felt the few times I'd passed out in my life or came close to passing out. Oh God, please don't let me faint I prayed to a deity I made up for this brief request. I pressed harder against the white wall, willing myself to remain upright with the living rather than supine with the corpses. I became aware of people standing now. *Oh good*, I thought, *they're all offering me a seat. What polite young gentlemen. And what nice young women to offer an older woman their seats.* Then, I realized the class was over. I put a knee on an empty chair to steady myself, pretending that I was just being cool. My dizziness was gone, I no longer felt numb. I took a few deep breaths and thanked the deity for her benevolence. It must be the formaldehyde, I thought.

Back at home, the family gave me a recap from Cassie's preschool teacher's visit. "Nice," said Cassie. "Nice," said Rachel. "She seemed nice," said Martin. It bothered me that I wasn't there, but the family seemed fine with my absence.

Chapter 6

AUGUST TO
SEPTEMBER 1985

The following day began our months-long dive into anatomy. Our table assignments were alphabetical—the common element to our cadaver table was the first letter of our last names. Most groups were all male. Our group had two women and two men. I felt relieved to have another woman to work with. We wore the required safety goggles, which made it difficult to read emotions on each other's faces. *Good*, I thought, *they won't be able to see the terror in my eyes*. Our white lab coats and plastic gloves were to protect us from the chemicals and any remaining bodily fluids from our cadaver. What would protect us, I wondered, from the soul of this dead person lashing out at the desecration of her body? Would she visit us in our dreams later, punishing us for looking at her nakedness, cutting into her?

The smell of formaldehyde was overpowering. I could feel it permeate my pores. I felt possessed. Industrial-size sinks lined one wall of the lab. A few skeletons stood sentry in the corners, hanging from rolling carts, watching us. The tables were cold silver steel. We stood at attention around our cadaver while the anatomy professor told us what would be expected of us. I dreaded the moment when we would remove the sheet and see the corpse. I dreaded having to touch her cold skin, even with the protective barrier of the plastic gloves. I wished I had worn two pairs of gloves.

I was no stranger to dead people. As a child, I'd attended many Irish-Catholic wakes and funerals with my mother and aunt. The wakes were open-casket, with the dead person laid out in peaceful repose, makeup providing a rosy glow. We would walk up to the casket, kneel down next to the body, bless ourselves, say a prayer, and look at the dead person. I would concentrate on the deceased's hands that invariably clutched a rosary as if praying for salvation. Other relatives would touch those hands, and the close relatives—wives, children, siblings—would lean in to kiss the person's cheek. My stomach would turn at the sight. I couldn't touch a corpse. I hadn't even touched the dead body of my beloved granduncle Jake, who had called me Miss Boston and spoiled me with bakery cupcakes.

Now I'd have to touch a dead person.

The instructor told us to remove the plastic cover, taking care not to spray preservatives into the air, to fold the cover neatly, and place it on the shelf under the table. At the end of each lab, we were to re-cover the body with this plastic cover. I took a few seconds to examine our cadaver head to toe. Her gray hair was long and straggly; formaldehyde was not a good hair product. Her body was thin and elderly. No cosmetics made her look better, no rosary comforted her on her journey to the next life, no weeping relatives stood by her. I wondered what had caused her death. Our cadaver was my first patient. But I couldn't save her. She at least had a long life, I realized.

We would take turns dissecting our cadaver, one person per lab session. The scalpel-yielding person would stand to the body's right side and follow the teacher's instructions. We would be graded on the quality of our dissections. If one of us made a mess, the rest of us would suffer. On this first lab day, I happened to be standing on the cadaver's right side, near her arm. This put me in the initial dissecting position, as we were to begin with the arm. I felt petrified to start, but relieved to have my first attempt over early. I wished I had read the required text pages on dissection how-to. My hand shook as I aimed the scalpel down. Slowly, I lowered it to the body.

"What are you doing?" our instructor demanded into my left ear. I jumped, and the knife clattered out of my hand onto the steel table. Clearly a surgical career wasn't in my future. I fumbled to retrieve the instrument while stammering a response. My tablemates looked on, wide-eyed, probably relieved not to be in my position right then.

"You need to read the assigned text before it's your turn to dissect," the instructor said. She proceeded to show me what I should have been doing. She didn't seem to be a cruel woman. but she could have been warm and fuzzy, and I'd still have been terrified of her. I was that on-edge, with the dead bodies, the required reading which I had no time to do, the pressure to learn the entirety of human biology, and the competition from other, smarter, younger students.

I could tell that this class would not be an easy pass.

The first months of medical school focused on structure and function of the human body. Gross Anatomy, or macroscopic anatomy, is the study of the body with what you can see with your naked eye. And true to its name, a full study of gross anatomy included time in the laboratory dissecting a dead body. Histology, or microscopic anatomy, was the study of tissues and cells, as seen under a microscope.

Thrown into intensive anatomy lectures and laboratories, we'd learn to identify the name and function of every body part. We'd study how one body part was connected to another body part. We would understand and speak a new language. We sweated in our axillae instead of armpits.

We ambulated instead of walking. We sat on a coccyx instead of a tailbone. We'd learn the names and locations of the 206 bones in the human body and the over 650 muscles that support those bones along with tendons and ligaments. We'd study the structure and function of the body's organs, nervous system, and blood and lymph systems. And to make sure that we learned all of this, the professors would test us frequently with a grueling exam schedule.

We also had a Clinical Medicine course that lasted the entire year. There were different modules, such as learning how to do a general physical exam and how to perform specific tests. For the physical exam tutorial, I was paired with another female medical student, and we were assigned to a female attending physician. This worked well, as we were not embarrassed about performing intimate exams such as the breast and pelvic areas. Later, the same student and I were assigned to a practicing community physician to learn how to interview patients about their current concerns and how to write up a full medical history. I loved this class because I learned how to interact with patients and how physicians think and work. I almost felt like a doctor.

Even though the labs were designed for group work, and many students studied together, we all knew that there was competition among us. While the grades were pass/fail, there was also the "H" grade. It stood for "honor." People with a lot of "H" grades would breeze through medical school with attending doctors and other students knowing they had this distinction. Perhaps the "H" should have represented "halo," to show the righteousness of these honor students. Their holiness would follow them into the third and fourth-year clinical work and would help them enter the pearly gates of a prestigious residency and subsequent fellowship program. I received no "Hs" in my first two years.

On my drive home, I'd think less and less about medicine, and more and more about the girls and Martin. By the time I reached the halfway point, I turned into an ordinary suburban housewife driving her station wagon to pick up her preschooler at the Montessori school in Yorktown and meet her seven-year-old sister at the school bus stop. This was the best part of my day—seeing the girls, taking care of them, playing with them. Things would get dicey with the evening crush of preparing supper, eating, cleaning up, supervising baths, and assisting with bedtime routines. Then there was the endless reading and studying. But the couple of afternoon hours were an oasis of joy.

Classes, labs, reading, memorizing, classes, labs, reading, memorizing. So went the first three weeks of medical school, and before I knew it our initial set of "block" exams were upon us. They were called "block" exams because they would test us on the most recent block of material in each class. In anatomy, they'd cover the musculoskeletal system. There would be a multiple-choice paper and pencil test, plus an anatomy lab practicum that would involve identifying specimens laid out on lab tables. Histology/cell biology would cover the first five chapters of an enormous text.

The school assigned each medical student a three-foot laminated wood carrel in one of several study rooms. Thirty or so cubicles lined the perimeter of the room. The carrels were allocated alphabetically, so the students to either side of me were Mc's, just like in my predominantly Irish-American Boston Catholic grade school. Here we studied, peered down microscope necks to distinguish tiny things such as blood cells in our histology lab, and took our exams.

These were not just run-of-the-mill tests to determine whether you've mastered the material. These were brutal, rip-your-guts-out exams. These separated the haves from the have-nots, the future doctors from the flunkies. Our first-year schedule included regular exams every three to four weeks in each of our science classes.

Stories circulated of people who flunked out of medical school or who had to repeat a year. The threat of failure hung heavy over my head, filling me with dread. I had dragged my family 3,000 miles across the country so that I could enter the golden kingdom of doctorhood to be one of the chosen. If I failed, it would mean I'd put my family through that for nothing. We'd never regain the financial losses we sustained by the move because even if I did land a research job, I'd never command a physician-level salary. And there would be the shame—how could I show my face to anyone if I flunked?

On exam day, I sat in my assigned cubicle, legs bouncing to release pent-up tension. The proctor took his sweet time handing out the histology test booklets—I was convinced that the time lag would handicap me. My anxiety ratcheted up to pure terror after I received my test and I realized the exam questions were not about the concepts and facts the teacher had presented in class, nor about the information from the lecture handouts. Instead, they were taken from the textbook's footnotes, the unimportant asides that you only look at if you're reading for fun. The "for examples" I glanced over as I memorized the main points. And even I, with no clinical experience, could tell that very few of the questions had anything to do with medicine, disease, or health. Head bent over the exam, I felt the carrel close in on me like a cheap coffin. In my own little hell, it was me against the ogre test booklet and its evil sister, the bubble-in answer sheet.

The first question on the histology/cell biology test stopped me cold. There were six possible answers, "a" through "f," and you had to choose the best answer: 1) a, d, and f; 2) b, d, and e; 3) b and c; 4) a and e; or e) a, b, c, e, and f. I had to think carefully about which ones could not possibly be true and which ones were definitely true, and then choose the best combination of answers. One or two of these on an exam would be challenging enough. But most of the questions were in this format. I struggled through the test, blindly guessed on some answers, handed in my sweaty answer sheet, and worried about the anatomy test that would follow in fifteen minutes. During the break, students gathered together in groups. I heard several ask others "What did you put for . . . ?" Some groups were laughing—they must have been the smart ones, who knew all the answers and found the tests to be fun. I spent half the break in the ladies' room and returned early to my carrel, hoping to calm my nerves. After two more exams that morning—anatomy and anatomy lab—I was released for the day. Later, I stewed over the questions. I vowed not to look up answers, for fear of discovering my errors. I was convinced that I'd failed all three, that I'd have to admit my shortcomings to Martin, and that I'd flunk out of medical school in the first year.

Over the next few days, I fretted until the grades were posted on long white reams of computer paper outside our study room. I'd passed, but my scores were just a couple of points above the passing level of 70 percent. It was too close for comfort. I vowed to study more. I just didn't know where I'd find the time.

One morning, as we waited in the auditorium for class to start, a nearby student noticed me glancing at a booklet in front of him.

"I'm studying for my driving test," he explained.

"Oh," I said, surprised. He looked much older than sixteen years old, the age when I'd gotten my driver's license.

"I've lived in the city all my life. None of my friends know how to drive. We don't need to, and no one wants a car in the city."

"Wow. I didn't realize that." I had grown up in a city too—Boston— but everyone I knew learned to drive at age sixteen. The boys had to drive their dates, if their dads let them use the family car. The girls had to drive to run errands for their mothers.

"Yeah but living up here in Westchester I have to be able to drive to get to my hospital assignments. It's an incredible pain. Here I am trying to study for our exams, and I have to take time to learn to drive also."

I thought about this. I recalled learning to drive as a teenager. It wasn't particularly time consuming then, and I doubted it would be much different for this guy. And compared with the time sink of mothering, it would be a breeze to just take a few driving lessons, brush through the driving rule booklets, and take a driving test. I wondered how he'd handle getting kids ready for school in the morning, picking them up after school, feeding and bathing them, reading to them, playing games with them, taking them to doctor's appointments and lessons, staying up all night when they were sick.

I just smiled at him, not sure how to tell him how easy his medical school experience looked in comparison with mine.

I wanted to belong; I needed a tribe. Everything about medical school and New York felt foreign. I sat every day with a room full of almost 200 other medical students, eyes riveted on one professor after another as they droned on about their particular subject that was so critical to our education. There were no other moms among my medical student class. There was one dad. He and I shared a wild-eyed look when we talked about taking care of kids while trying to cram thousands of facts into our heads and retain them as if we were ten years younger. But his wife did most of the childcare. And a dad taking care of kids is not the same as a mom taking care of kids. First, there's the guilt factor, or, in the case of dads, the lack of guilt factor. Dads get points just for being present, and if they do things like take kids to lessons, make supper, and laundry, they are treated like they walk on water. Whereas if women neglect to do those things, they are labelled Bad Moms.

By 1985, the proportion of women in medical school classes had grown to about a third, as it was in New York Medical College. So, I had plenty of female colleagues to bond with. They were just all a decade younger than I, without family responsibilities. Oh, we had worries in common about mastering material and passing exams. But outside of medicine, they focused heavily on dating and finding life partners. I focused on the girls' and Martin's schedules and needs, keeping the house clean, taking the girls to the mall for school clothes and supplies, and dealing with the many other things that moms do.

I wanted another mom to talk with, to ask how she handled classes, studying, and mothering. I wanted to tell her how I felt guilty when I didn't volunteer to assist on my daughters' class field trips, when I purchased cookies for a bake sale instead of making them, when my husband took the kids to a park on a Saturday morning, all so I could study. I wanted to say how guilty I felt that with all this accommodation my family made to allow me to study, I wasn't doing all that great on the tests. As if I should excel to atone for my family's sacrifices. I wanted to hear another mom tell me she had the same problems and worried about the same things.

In retrospect, it's not surprising that there were no other mothers in the class. Medical training was first developed when only men became doctors. The schedule is grueling. In the first two years, full days of classes are followed by hours of study at night and weekends. Then come two clinical years, where students spend long days and nights working in hospitals. And that's the easy part. Any physician who wants to practice in the US must complete a residency, ranging from three to five years. Some specialties require fellowship training after residency. As a result, most new doctors are in their early- to mid- thirties before they are fully qualified to work as physicians.

CHAPTER 6

The few female doctors in the generations before me were anomalies— there might be one or two women in a class, and they had to shoulder the same workload as the men. Since women in that era were responsible for childcare, a woman couldn't possibly handle being both a student and a mother. Many of the women physicians never married; perhaps they couldn't see having a medical career and children for the same reasons they couldn't handle the load as students. Or maybe they weren't considered to be attractive mates, given their choice to enter a competitive field that belonged to men. Some may not have wanted to marry for reasons of their own. As a result, there weren't many women who were both physicians and moms. I didn't see any role models. I had no one to show me how it's done.

Chapter 7

OCTOBER TO

NOVEMBER 1985

One early October morning, several students huddled at the back of class at 8:25 a.m.—Histology/Cell Biology would begin in five minutes. I couldn't see what was happening behind the crush of jeans and designer sweatshirts. Then my friend Kathy emerged from the crowd, laughing and clutching a white sheet of paper. She and I had met in the back of class, when she asked to see my notes. We had nothing in common: she was ten years younger than I, single, beautiful, and popular. I was honored that she'd even talk to me.

"Annie," she said, "you have to get in on this."

"What is it?" I asked.

"It's Squingo. You pay a dollar for a playing sheet."

"Huh?"

"Squingo. Shit, class is starting. I'll tell you about it after."

We took our seats as the Cell Biology professor began to drone. As usual, I sat three rows from the back, on the aisle, the closest seat to the auditorium's door. I wanted the quickest escape route, as if a physical route of easy egress could make the stress of medical school on top of motherhood any easier. At 9:15, ten minutes before the end of class, the professor asked if there were any questions. Several hands from the first few rows shot up. The professor called on one, and the student asked a question.

"Yes!" came a whisper in the row behind me. A low murmur rose from another section of the room.

"Any more questions?"

Additional questions were asked and answered. The class was more restive than usual. This same pattern occurred through the next lecture. Then, suddenly, right before the mid-morning break, a student shouted, "Squingo!" The professor asked, "Excuse me?" Several students groaned, and others laughed.

I found Kathy during the break and asked what was going on. She was laughing so hard she could barely talk. She pulled me aside, away from the group of students we had been standing near.

"Some of the kids set up a game. Each piece of paper has pictures of the squids arranged in different patterns, like a Bingo card. You pay one dollar for a game. Here's my card."

I looked at her game sheet. Twenty grainy black and white pictures of medical students looked up at us, some smiling.

"What's a squid?" I asked.

"Oh Annie, you're not with it. You're concentrating too hard on being a mommy. The nerds who sit at the front of the class are called 'squids.' Haven't you noticed that they're the only ones who ask questions? In Squingo, each time a squid asks a question in class, you make a mark on that person's picture. The first person to mark off all the squids in a row wins the pot of money."

"But why are they called squids?"

"It's got something to do with a neurobiology class from years ago. The professor talked about the nervous system of a squid every day for the entire semester. The smart kids who sat up front asked the most stupid questions about the creatures. The rest of the class started calling them squids."

The pictures were arranged in four neat rows. I recognized several of the older students. They were delightful people, serious about the new careers they were embarking on as adults, and would make wonderful doctors. That they were the target of ridicule gave me a small jolt of distaste. Still, I didn't chastise my friend. The sheer brilliance of the scheme awed me. I wanted to be clever like the "cool" students who had invented Squingo. That Kathy, a key member of the "in" crowd was my friend and let me in on this secret game was a major coup for me. I was usually the little girl in the playground with her thumb in her mouth watching the other kids play, not joining in, because she doesn't know how to fit in.

"Where did you all get these pictures?" I asked.

"One of the guys works in the admissions office and made copies of the squids' photos. Then some of the girls cut out the photos, arranged them randomly on twenty Squingo sheets, and glued them on."

"Do those guys know that they're on the Squingo cards?"

"Yeah, and they were really pissed about it. I think today's will be the last game. Too bad you didn't get the chance to play, Annie."

The perpetrators didn't stop with making fun at the expense of other students. They also targeted teachers. One morning, a clutch of students stood at the back of the auditorium with their heads together. They mostly whispered, but an occasional guffaw escaped. They sat down when the histology professor said from the front, "Okay, let's begin now." Today's lecture was on blood—white blood cells, red blood cells, and platelets. White blood cells included several subtypes: neutrophils, lymphocytes, monocytes, basophils, and eosinophils. There were subsets of these subtypes. For example, lymphocytes include natural killer cells, T-lymphocytes and B-lymphocytes. Each of these subtypes had subtypes.

The blood cells all looked different, had different contents, and varying functions. We had to know it all.

"Let me schematize this for you," the professor said as she proceeded to draw on the blackboard. She drew a circle with a three-foot radius. Inside she drew another circle, twice the size of her head. She erased the inner circle and instead drew something that looked like three fat sausage links connected with strings. Next to the cell she wrote "Neutrophil." She talked about neutrophils and how they fight infections. She talked about what an immature neutrophil might look like under the microscope. She described how doctors and technicians look at structure and numbers of neutrophils, to determine health of the blood. My mind drifted a little, but a murmur from the back of the room brought me back to attention. The professor was now talking about lymphocytes, and she had drawn another big circle, this time with very large circle inside it. "I've schematized this cell," she said, "so you can clearly see how different it looks from a neutrophil." I heard twitters from the back of the hall.

The teacher talked and drew, talked and drew, for the rest of the period. Close to the end of class, she said, "Our time is up today. Tomorrow I'll schematize the other white blood cells."

Suddenly, a medical student stood up, raised his fist, and said, "I got it!"

"What, schematize?" the professor asked. The student groaned and sat down. Laughter and clapping erupted from the seats around him.

After class, my friend filled me in on what had happened. This professor was famous for her use of the word "schematize." The students had placed bets on how many times she would say the word during this morning's lecture. The student who stood and shouted had just won the bet by guessing there would be twenty-one occasions of the word. But when she asked, "What, schematize?" the number went to twenty-two, and he lost to another player.

❦

Then I learned about the parties. The medical students played as hard as they studied. After each set of block exams, they would celebrate. As most of the students lived in Grasslands, the medical student dormitory, the parties were held there. I wished I could attend, countering the stresses of studying with infusions of cheap alcohol. But for me, this would not be as simple as sauntering down from my dorm room. It would involve getting Martin interested in going to what was a step above a frat party. We'd have to hire and pay a babysitter, and then feed and settle the girls for the night. Then we'd have to drive the half hour down to Valhalla, a trip I already made five times a week and didn't want to repeat without strong need. One or both of us would need to severely limit our drinking. We never did go to one of the dorm parties.

However, the students and the school hosted some more sophisticated events, real cocktail parties instead of beer blasts. Martin and I attended several. I drank too much and pretty much made a fool of myself. But I fit in with the younger students who were even more impaired than I. It didn't take much to make me inebriated because given my mom duties and studying schedule, I never drank more than half a beer in an evening. I had little physical tolerance for booze.

This was not the first time I'd overindulged in alcohol. I had my first alcohol-induced blackout at age seventeen, early in my freshman year at Emmanuel College in Boston. An older student procured Ripple wine for us and most likely made a profit on what she charged us. I guzzled down most of a quart and woke up in my bed the next morning with little memory of what happened the previous night. According to my less-inebriated friends, all of my drunk behavior occurred right in my dorm room, so I avoided the kinds of trouble that drunk women can face.

I didn't realize that I'd had a blackout, just thought I'd gone to sleep. Soon, my girlfriends and I ventured on Friday and Saturday nights down Longwood Avenue to the sleazy bars in Kenmore Square. We'd pay a small cover charge and then rely on guys inside to pay for our watered-down beer. Those same guys would pinch our butts as we squeezed through a crowd on our way to the ladies' room. I drank to have courage to talk with those guys, to quell my fears of my own sexuality, and perhaps to deaden the pain of the ass-pinching. I'd stumble out with my friends, luckily making it back to the safety of the college dorm. We complained bitterly about the curfew imposed by our Catholic college dormitory but, in retrospect, it probably kept me out of some trouble.

Now back in the role of student, I wanted to be accepted by the cool kids. I looked young for my thirty-two years. When a cute male student asked where I lived, I responded, "With my family in Yorktown," knowing full well that he would not realize "family" meant husband and children. What was I thinking? I wasn't looking for a relationship outside of my marriage. It was as if I thought that by being single and young, I could erase the difficulties of medical school. The stresses of being both mother and student were overwhelming.

Looking back, I can see clearly that there were significant advantages to my being an older, married student with children. First, my family provided me with warmth, affection, and security. My husband was incredibly supportive. The girls gave me unconditional love. Second, since I lived with people I loved, I didn't have to deal with finding compatible roommates. Third, I was financially stable. IBM paid Martin a generous salary, so we didn't have to worry about making the mortgage payments. Finally, the children kept me grounded: I had to be present for them, which somewhat reduced the amount of time I could ruminate about the likelihood of failing.

Perhaps I thought that if I was one of the group, their smartness would rub off on me. I certainly wasn't succeeding at absorbing all the knowledge being crammed into us. My friend Kathy tried to teach me some anatomy mnemonics.

"It's easy," Kathy said when I'd complained about trying to memorize bones and other anatomy structures. "So, for the wrist bones you just remember 'Some Lovers Try Positions That They Can't Handle.' The first letter of each word corresponds to the first letter of a bone. The bones are Scaphoid, Lunate, Triquetrum, Pisiform, Trapezium, Trapezoid, Capitate, Hamate." She went on to describe several raunchy mnemonics for other anatomical structures. I wondered why so many of the mnemonics involved the female genitalia, prostitutes, and sex acts. It probably reflected the male-dominance of the profession. I didn't want to commit these to memory—I'd be stuck with them in my head without really remembering the anatomy structures. Kathy had no trouble remembering either the sentences or the names of the structures.

I felt like the slow kid in the class, the one who would need to repeat kindergarten. But this wasn't kids' play. It was a big-bucks, big-stakes endeavor.

Meanwhile, the girls were settling in very well with their new schools and friends. Seven-year-old Rachel was in second grade at Brookside Elementary public school in Yorktown Heights. Rachel excelled at school, and the teachers were very good at finding material to challenge her. She also was developing several friendships, although her angst of fitting in mirrored that of my concern with blending with the medical students. Only for her, it was normal. For me, a grown woman and mother of two, it was odd.

Cassie attended the Montessori preschool in Yorktown. She thrived there, loved her teachers, and developed close friendships with several girls. She adored her older sister, though, and looked forward to their afternoons together. If Rachel had a friend over, Cassie wanted in on the action. If the older girls tried to exclude Cassie, the resulting trauma and drama required a lot of love and attention from the supervising parent.

Yorktown Heights is one of five hamlets in the town of Yorktown, a forty-square-mile rectangle in northwestern Westchester County with a population of 37,500. It consists largely of single-family homes—raised ranches, split-levels, Cape Cods and colonials, and some pre-Revolutionary homes. It has amenities, like the Turkey Mountain Nature Preserve and the Franklin D. Roosevelt State Park that my husband and I would make frequent use of now as active older adults. However, we spent most of our leisure time on the girls' activities: arranging and supervising play dates, and driving to and from piano, ballet, gymnastics, swimming, and horseback lessons.

My exhaustion from the late-night studying made getting up in the mornings challenging. Martin rose at the first sound of his alarm. After a quick shower, he took charge of the girls' breakfast. I managed to get myself washed and dressed, and then began hunting for the girls' missing items: socks, Sealie for Cassie, a favorite book for Rachel. Martin would walk Rachel down to her bus, and I'd gather Cassie into the car and drop her at her preschool on my way to my own school. If one of her friends was there, she'd happily run off to play with her. If not, she'd cling to me and I'd have to enlist the help of a teacher to distract her long enough for me to escape. More days than not I'd be late for class.

One morning I missed my regular entrance to the medical school and had to continue around to the back entrance, past the Westchester County Jail. There were so many similarities between the jail and the medical school, I realized. Both had red brick buildings. Several of the medical school buildings were early 1900s county structures originally used for various treatments—psychiatry, tuberculosis, malnourished children. The county jail had been housed on the campus for almost a century and expanded over time.

But the similarities went beyond the buildings. The internees were not in control of what they did: prisoners had regimens to follow, medical students were required to attend classes and take exams. They were forced to listen to their superiors: inmates heed the guards, students had to listen in lectures. They wore uniforms: prison garb for inmates, white coats for medical students. There was little choice in who they spent their time with: prisoners were assigned cell mates and work details; medical students were assigned lab partners. Labor was largely unpaid, although most medical students could be assured of a decent wage in future years. The institutional stays were temporary, so people counted the years, months, and days until their release. The world expected both the students and the prisoners to be better people at the end of their stints. Then, once released, the public would think they were stealing from them. Life was stressful for both.

I felt like a prisoner as I approached the school that morning. I forgot my original excitement at being granted admission to the private club of physicians and felt obligated to endure whatever Medicine threw at me. I was being punished for my choice of going to medical school: I had to do my time.

Chapter 8

DECEMBER 1985

I sat in a small classroom with nine other students, looking at breasts. These were not real breasts, and they weren't attached to women. Rather, they were models, made of some sort of thick, pliable plastic. The only similarity between these breasts and real ones were that these were of different sizes and, I'd soon discover, different consistencies. They were all a sickly pink color. Perhaps the makers tried to emulate white breasts, forgetting that most of the women in the world have breasts of color. But as it turned out, this class would be all about feeling. It didn't matter what color these ugly things were, and we could have done our feeling with our eyes closed.

Our teacher today—a nurse—pointed to a picture of a breast on an easel and described the correct way to palpate a breast. Our task was to learn how to find lumps so that we could later apply the technique to real women, our patients. The clinical breast exam to screen for breast cancer was part of a routine physical for women. The breast exam was also performed for women who present with breast symptoms that could indicate cancer.

This class didn't worry me. First, as a woman, this was not a foreign body part to me. Second, as a mom who had nursed as recently as two years prior, I was comfortable with feeling breasts. I had determined which breast still had some milk in it—by poking around—because I could never remember which side my baby had last drained.

On the nurse's cue, we stood around a table in front of ten models. We were to feel each one, find the lumps (if any), and identify the location. Then we would indicate the lump and its estimated size on a paper drawing of a breast with clock numbers around a circle. We'd move around the table until we had palpated all ten models. The nurse would review our findings. The task felt like finding rocks inside Play-Doh; none of the models felt like my breasts. The male students seemed perplexed and needed extra help. The female students did a little better but took their time. In less than ten minutes I correctly identified the lumps in the ten breast models. This made me happy for two reasons: I succeeded at something, and I could leave class early to go home. I could study for a half hour in the car until it was time to pick up Cassie at her preschool. Even the freezing December air wouldn't detract from my pleasure at having thirty minutes of stolen time for studying.

Riding high on my afternoon's success, I decided to try palpating my own breasts that night. Lying in bed, I performed a self-exam. First, I examined the right breast. Smugly, I thought that I could easily do this exam on real breasts. Then, to my surprise and horror, I found a lump in my left breast at the 3 o'clock position, the outermost part of the breast. The lump was pea-sized, about a centimeter in diameter, and hard. There were no other lumps in either breast. I slept little that night, convinced that I now had breast cancer and that would be the end of me.

After classes the next day, I rushed over to the students' medical clinic, where a young attending confirmed that I did indeed have a pea-sized mass. He referred me right away to a surgeon, who agreed to see me the next day. The surgeon, a gruff but gentle man, also confirmed the mass, ordered a mammogram, and said I'd need a biopsy regardless of what the mammogram showed. Biopsies in 1985 were done surgically, in an operating room. He kindly worked around my class schedule. My biopsy would be done the day after Christmas. Oh great, I thought, I'll have a lovely holiday with this event looming. I felt a little guilty that this scheduled biopsy could also be interfering with the doctor's holiday plans.

Convinced that I had breast cancer, and that it would quickly kill me, I stewed in worry. I was sure that I'd leave my young girls without a mother. The thought of not being around to care for my little ones badgered me. While they had a wonderful, involved dad, they needed mom for quick hugs, wiping away tears, and providing comfort against nighttime terrors.

That night, I told Martin about the breast lump, my appointment with the surgeon, and the mammogram. I hadn't wanted to tell him— verbalizing made it seem more real.

"It will be fine," he said.

How did he know? If he was right, why did the surgeon feel a need to cut me open? Martin had been only six years old when his mother had her first breast cancer. The family claimed that her two boys weren't bothered by her two-week absence. Was Martin's nonchalance because his mother had survived her breast cancer? Or perhaps, a true mathematician, he knew the odds of my having breast cancer at age thirty-two were low. His simple statement that things would be fine didn't convince me.

My term ended the same day as did the girls' classes—Friday, December 20—and Martin could also take time off. We'd have a ten-day break together. Ordinarily, I'd be ecstatic about the additional time with my family. But this holiday would be different.

First, my mother and Aunt Margie would be arriving on the twenty-first. They would drive from Plymouth, Massachusetts by car. The trip, normally a three-and-a-half-hour drive, would take them six hours. My mother would do all the driving, in the white sedan my aunt had bought years earlier in the hopes that she'd finally learn to drive. Twenty-five years before this, Margie had failed her road test three times in a row. The car sat in her driveway waiting for her to repeat her driving test, which she never did. My mother drove it occasionally to keep it running.

On the way to Yorktown Heights, Margie would need a cigarette every hour. They'd both need several coffee and bathroom breaks. They'd stop for a clam roll along the Connecticut shore. And, because Margie feared busy highways, they'd take it slower: Route 44 West from Plymouth, connecting to Route 6 West in Providence, and then several small roads through Connecticut. They'd arrive tired and cranky.

The two sisters were close; they lived one town apart and talked by phone every day. But put the two of them in proximity for several hours and a battle was sure to break out. Their fights involved sniping and bickering. Often, one of them would initiate the silent treatment. When I was a child, they used me as the go-between during their silent treatment periods. As in, "Anne, tell your mother that . . . " If my mother was the instigator, I'd be expected to take her side and avoid talking with Margie unless I had to deliver some important message. It was insanity-inducing.

While I desperately wanted my girls to experience the benefits of an extended family and desired this for myself, I dreaded every visit from my mother and aunt. This time would be worse than usual; the terror of the upcoming biopsy along with the stress of medical school would limit my defenses against the visitors' moods and behaviors. The one advantage of the timing would be that my mother and aunt could babysit the girls while Martin took me to the hospital for my biopsy. Although, I'd have to worry about how they were treating the girls. Margie tended to be kind and full of fun with the girls, so I was less concerned about her. However, my mother could turn nasty on a slight provocation, and I feared that she would hit them as she had done so often to me. I had given her strict instructions in the past never to hit the girls, and she promised to comply. I just didn't trust her.

As expected, my mother and aunt arrived Saturday evening right before supper. Both groaned as they emerged from the car. They had shrunk over the years. My mother's dowager's hump brought her height several inches lower than in her young adult years, and she was now shorter than I. Her gray hair, recently permed, curled tight to her head. She wore a peach-hued jersey blouse and white polyester pants. Her clothing was pristine despite the long journey but stretched across her considerable girth. She smelled of Estee Lauder's latest cologne.

Half a dozen bobby pins barely contained Margie's thick white hair, which she trimmed herself with dull scissors. I shuddered inside, knowing some of the bobby pins would fall out in my house. Margie used these as tools, such as scraping the last bit of red lipstick from its holder to "use it up." Her glasses made her dark brown eyes look larger. Always a short woman, she had recently grown thick around the waist. She clutched her ever-present overstuffed black leather purse.

"Hello, my Anna Banana," said Margie as she hugged me firmly, her head coming no higher than my chin. "You look beautiful as always," she continued. She smelled of stale cigarette smoke.

"Your face is a mess, I see," my mother said, inspecting with her small brown eyes my recurring perioral dermatitis, a rash around my mouth that invariably showed up for her visits.

The girls were excited to see them. Cassie jumped up and down and gave the ladies big hugs. Rachel hung back at first but allowed herself to be embraced. The girls showed them to where they would be sleeping: my mother to the guest bedroom, Aunt Margie to the sofa bed in the downstairs family room. During supper, we heard about the drive and about my mother's husband and neighbors. She didn't ask the girls or me about our school, friends, lives.

The next morning, I took my mother, aunt, and daughters to the 9:00 Sunday Mass at St. Patrick's Catholic Church. It was the first time I'd been to church in many years. I took the group because I knew Margie would be frantic if she couldn't go to weekly Mass, and I thought it could be instructive for the girls to see a church service. While my mother could not take Communion because of her divorce and remarriage, she still attended Mass, so I knew she'd also appreciate this. During the service, Rachel read a book she'd snuck into her pocket. Cassie squirmed over and under the pew. After returning home, we ate a brunch that Martin had prepared while we were out.

In the middle of the meal, my mother stated, "I want to see a New York show tonight. Maybe the Rockettes."

I took a deep breath. We lived an hour from the city in good traffic.

"You'll need to call Radio City Hall for tickets. If you can even get tickets this time of year at the last minute." I paused, then added, "It'll take you about an hour to get to the city. Martin can give you directions."

My mother narrowed her eyes and thrust out her chin. "I would hope my daughter could take care of this for me. After all I've done for you, and now driving all the way from Plymouth to see you and your little brats."

Margie looked nervously from one of us to the other but remained quiet. Rachel began to cry. Cassie asked, "Mom, what's a brat?"

"Come on, girls, let's go play in your room." I felt badly about leaving Martin with my mother and aunt, but I knew he could handle my mother's vitriol better than the girls or I.

My mother's demand didn't surprise me. On a trip to Seattle when I was pregnant with Cassie, my mother announced that she wanted to see Vancouver Island in British Columbia during her stay. I made the mistake of obliging her by taking her and then three-year-old Rachel on a grueling trip while nauseous and exhausted. The journey included four hours of driving, an hour-long ferry, and a border crossing just to get to Victoria, the southernmost point. She wanted to see Nanaimo, another two-hour trip north from Victoria. Halfway through the tour my mother complained that none of the trip was for her, that I spent all my time taking care of Rachel. I vowed to myself to never again cater to my mother at the expense of my children.

Later, after the girls were in bed, I told my mother and aunt about my upcoming breast biopsy.

With a sharp intake of air, Margie said, "Oh dear Lord."

My mother said, "Thank God I've never had to deal with breast cancer."

My mother's reaction hurt deep under my breast, with a pain no amount of surgery or treatment could cure. This was why I never bothered to tell her about any illness I experienced. Once she called me when I had the flu. I doubled over coughing after saying, "Hello." "You sound terrible," my mother said on the other end. I responded with more coughing. She then launched into a detailed description of her symptoms with the flu the previous year, complete with what she coughed up and blew out, the daily fluctuations in her temperature, the overwhelming fatigue, and her lengthy recovery. After she finished I said I had to go and crawled back to the couch where I could oversee the girls' play with one eye open.

Over the years, I'd wanted to distance myself from my mother. The 3,000 miles between her home in Plymouth, Massachusetts, and my home in Seattle had not been enough to completely sever ties. I knew it would be upsetting for Margie if I broke off communication with my mother. Whenever I complained about my mother, Margie told me that I was lucky to have a mother at all. She and my mother had lost their own mother to cancer when they were twelve and seventeen years old. I also wanted my daughters to have an extended family. I had not known my own grandparents. Three had died by the time I was four years old, and my mother avoided her alcoholic father. Our girls had a chance to know family from the previous generation. I thought it would benefit the girls to have more people care about them, maybe even love them.

But another reason stopped me from cutting off relations with my mother. I didn't want to be the bad daughter. On several occasions, she had told me I was ungrateful for all she had done for me. "You should get down on your knees and beg God's forgiveness for how you've treated me," she'd said. If I was a bad daughter, people would assume I was a bad person. As if in atonement, I pretended to want to see her; I dutifully called her once a week and listened to her describe her physical ailments and her complaints about her miserable husband and their neighbors who were either snooty or low-class. I continued to arrange family holiday get-togethers and hoped that the girls would benefit from the interactions.

It boiled down to my fearing how it would reflect on me if I took care of my own need for distancing myself from my mother. Each time I spoke with her, each time I saw her, I recalled her screaming and hitting and slapping and threatening to send me away again. Even as a thirty-two-year-old adult, with a nice strong husband to protect me, I feared my mother. I was still afraid that she would strike me hard enough to cause injury. I worried that she'd find some way to send me away to an institution, tearing me apart from my husband and daughters. I thought she could kill me.

Children make Christmas special, and our girls were no exception. I loved seeing the girls' joy on Christmas morning. Cassie still believed in Santa, and Rachel very nicely played along with the pretense. (She might have been slightly influenced by the extra presents Santa brings.) Christmas morning was particularly magical for Margie. I suspect part of her wanted to believe that Santa really existed; her happiness that day almost matched that of our girls. My mother was more reserved than usual, although she did say she missed her husband. I was grateful that no fighting broke out between her and Margie.

I barely slept Christmas night. I had been instructed to arrive at the Westchester County Hospital at 7:00 a.m. for check-in and pre-op prep. The girls were awake to see us off. Both my mother and aunt had the look of fear in their eyes. I could tell that, like me, they assumed the worst. We'd told the girls that I would have a little operation on my breast.

"Will you die?" Rachel asked.

"No, of course not," I said. I hoped I sounded convincing.

Martin was chipper on the drive to Valhalla. "Everything will be fine," he said. Martin lived by math; since it was highly improbable that I had breast cancer at age thirty-two, he assumed I did not have breast cancer. I envied him his logical mind. I still envy this in him.

It felt odd to be driven into Grasslands Reservation, to the medical center. I worked hard to become a healer. I was not supposed to be the patient.

I shook throughout the pre-op activities. I told myself it was just the cold room, but I still shivered after the nurse gave me a warm blanket. I dreaded the news I knew I'd receive later that day. Martin stayed with me during this time but when the nurse came to bring me down to the operating room, he had to go to a waiting area. The nurse helped me up onto a gurney. I wasn't sure what to do. On TV, patients lie supine on gurneys. If the nurse had wanted me to sit, surely, she would have put me in a wheelchair. But I didn't feel sick enough to lie down. If I sat, I figured, I'd look less like a sick person. I made a quick choice. Sitting bolt-upright with my hospital gown flapping in back, I rode to the operating room. "Nice pre-op meds," quipped a passing nurse, referring to my unusual position. I hadn't realized that I could lie down, relax, and let these people take care of me.

The stark white hallway was punctuated by machinery, hurrying peopled dressed in scrubs, and long steel scrubbing sinks. The gurney stopped outside an operating room. On a white board, I saw my surgeon's name. Next to that were the initials "A.M." With a jolt, I realized I was first on that list. Inside the green-tiled operating room, my surgeon greeted me and introduced a young man as a third-year medical student who would be helping him. I felt some reluctance at another student being involved in my care but was happy to help with his education. However, when the nurses had me move over to the operating table and removed my hospital gown, I was not pleased to be stark naked in front of a peer. I hadn't had this sort of education in mind for him. Worried that he'd leer at my naked body, I looked over his way. I was relieved that he met my glance and did not look at my nudity.

Since a biopsy only required a local anesthetic, I remained awake through the procedure. I looked up at circular lights and round heads covered in surgical hats and masks. The surgeon stood to my left, the third-year student to my right. Nurses moved in and out of sight. The surgeon described the procedure in detail as he worked. He made the incision at the edge of the areola to reduce its later visibility, he said. At the time, I didn't care if it could be seen. I just didn't want it to be cancer. The student in me listened as the doctor taught. I hoped I'd live to be able to assist in an operation in the future. The procedure lasted about fifteen minutes; the surgeon sewed me up and left the room. The nurses busied themselves around me.

I barely had time to worry about the results when the surgeon came back into the room and hurried over to me. "Great news, Anne," he said. "The lump was just an adenoma, completely benign. You don't have cancer." He went on to explain that the pathologist looked at the frozen section to give a reading. The full pathology report would come back in about a week, but he expected the result to be the same. I felt my entire body relax in relief. I didn't have breast cancer. I wasn't going to die young, at least not likely, not right now. My girls wouldn't be left motherless.

The doctor told me to rest for the remainder of the day and to take it easy for the next week. I now had an excuse to stay in bed but I had to study for exams that were scheduled for the following week, right after New Year's. Back at home, I surrounded myself with textbooks. The girls piled onto my bed as well, with their own books. So much for concentrated study.

My mother and aunt left the day after my procedure. While I felt relief to see them go, I wanted them to stay to help me out. Not that they were the helping types but I wished they were. All my life, I'd fended for myself during illnesses. Even as young as seven or eight years of age, I stayed home alone when too sick to go to school. I remember dosing my sore throats with orange-flavored aspirin gum. With no one at home with me, I could use as much of this as I wanted. I loved the sweet orange taste. I'd learn in medical school that I could have ruined my kidneys with all that aspirin.

The doctor had bandaged my wound with strong surgical tape that pulled whenever I moved. Several other things pulled at me that week: the girls wanting mom to play with them, Martin needing help taking care of the girls, my breast trying to heal, my mind attempting to recover from the fear of cancer, and medical school demanding that I study and memorize for the upcoming tests. I was cramming too much into my little life.

It mattered nothing to my medical school that I'd just dealt with a potentially serious medical issue. While I was very lucky—many women don't get to hear those comforting words, "completely benign"—I was left shaken. Christmas vacation wasn't a real break when you're in medical school. By scheduling exams on the day that we returned, the school required a working holiday. While this could be annoying for some of the other students, for a mother juggling competing needs of children, husband, extended family, health, and medicine, it was daunting. This would require super-human concentration, but I was a mere mortal.

Looking back, I can see that I wasn't just dealing with physical illness. Circumstances were setting me up for considerable mental strain. I didn't realize that this could dwarf my physical issues. In 1985, there was no information readily available to medical students on how to deal with the stresses of school. There was no internet for searching information on problems, no social media for sharing thoughts and feelings. Nobody talked about doctors' mental health issues that can lead to addiction, failing practices, broken personal relations, or even suicide. No one talked about the high rate of suicide in physicians. Doctors were expected to be superheroes, able to function in brutal conditions. They were highly unlikely to seek help for mental illnesses because such illnesses could be cause for dismissal from training programs or jobs. Furthermore, many states required doctors to report current or previous mental illnesses and treatments, and medical boards could deny or revoke licenses for these conditions.

While my breast lump had turned out benign, I remained in a state that was anything but benign. I didn't know how I could continue. But I didn't know how to stop.

Chapter 9

DECEMBER 1985
TO JANUARY 1986

The day after my procedure, Martin offered to entertain the girls so I could have some studying time. Wanting to kiss his feet, I thanked him warmly. I shut myself away in our bedroom, bed piled with books, tea on my bed stand. I was deep into the cardiovascular system when the door opened with a crash. It was Cassie.

"Mommy, Daddy won't let me." She didn't get to finish.

"Let Mommy study," Martin said from behind her. He picked her up.

She struggled in his arms and yelled, "I want Mommy!"

He shut the door. I heard his footsteps down the hall, and then all was quiet. I knew that he could calm her down quickly—he just needed to think of a game to distract her from searching for Mommy. But nothing distracted me from thinking about how my little girl needed me and how I didn't deliver.

I am a horrible mother, I thought. I should have leapt right up when Cassie came into the room. I should have comforted her. I shouldn't have closeted myself away to study. I shouldn't have dragged my family across the country so I could go to medical school. I should have been happy with my life in Seattle as a faculty wife and mother.

Finally, I concentrated again on my anatomy notes. I had moved on to the structure of the heart with its valves and vessels when I smelled grilled cheese sandwiches cooking. Looking at the clock, I saw it was lunchtime. I joined my family and ate the sandwich crusts the girls discarded. Martin wanted to run errands, so I said I'd watch the girls.

I cleaned up the lunch dishes while I told the girls to go play together in the living room. Hopefully, they would keep busy with one of their games that involved draping blankets and comforters across the floor and furniture to make various geographical formations that they could then play in. I might be able to fit in thirty minutes' study time. My anatomy textbook sat on the kitchen counter, glowing red hot, calling me to open it. I dried my hands and reached my hand out to the book.

"Mommy, will you play with me?" Cassie asked from the doorway. Her curly red hair swirled around her head. She looked particularly cute.

"Where's Rachel? You were playing with her."

"She's reading a stupid book."

I sighed. My own books would have to wait. I hated that I felt so reluctant to play with my daughter. She must have noticed. Did she feel less important since I didn't jump right into play time with her? Would I scar her for life? Or should I tell her to find something to do on her own? Would that make her more self-reliant? (As it turns out, she grew into the most self-reliant woman I know. Something must have worked with my patchwork of motherhood.)

In my internal monologue, I tried to justify my preoccupation with studying. It will be good for my family in the long run, I reasoned.

On the morning of Tuesday, December 31, we loaded up the station wagon with the girls, various stuffed animals, kids' books, a dozen My Little Pony toys, four Barbie dolls, nice outfits for everyone including the Barbies, and headed south to Montclair, New Jersey. High school friends of Martin had invited us to a New Year's Eve party. We would stay overnight at their house. The girls would play with our hosts' children until bedtime, and then the adults would party with several of Martin's old high school friends. We'd stay the next morning for breakfast and socializing.

I didn't want to go. I was not prepared for the three exams coming up later that week. I could think of nothing other than the few hours of studying I could have been doing that day between activities with the girls. We could have plunked them down in front of a kids' movie. That would have given me ninety minutes. After they were asleep, I could perhaps have had another ninety minutes, maybe even two hours if the girls were cooperative at bedtime. I'd had little time to study over the past week. My Christmas "vacation" had been full of shopping and activities and kids and relatives and cooking and cleaning and having surgery to remove a breast lump and worrying about the lump before I knew it was benign. My breast scar wasn't completely healed—it had only been five days since I'd been sliced open—and it hurt when I moved. I hid it easily under a bandage, my bra, and an oversized cotton sweater I'd purchased on sale at the Jefferson Mall Sears. My stress, on the other hand, was a gaping wound. I hoped it didn't show.

Other medical students might have had some obligations during the break, maybe traveling to the family's Vermont ski chalet or perhaps they had flown to their parents' St. Bart's retreat. But their families would have understood if these young, single, future doctors went into quiet rooms to study for a few hours.

I felt reluctant to go for another reason. I felt outclassed. Martin had grown up in Bergenfield, New Jersey, a bedroom community of New York City. People in his town commuted to important financial jobs in the city. His dad was a vice president at the Guardian Life Insurance

Company. His friends, children of important people, had high-paying, high-class jobs. His best friend, with whom we would be staying, worked as a financial wizard at a large New York City bank. His wife, beautiful enough to have been a cheerleader, was an artist. Here I was, a peasant, lower-working-class, daughter of a single mother with no father, trying to mix with the upper classes. While my status had risen with my marriage to a university professor and climbed further now that Martin was at IBM Research, I worried that I wouldn't be accepted in his social circle. His friends would see right through the cheap veneer of my pretense. They'd know I belonged in the servants' quarters.

I'm sure that Martin would say that he and his friends had solid middle-class upbringings in solid middle-class neighborhoods in a solid middle-class town of Bergenfield, New Jersey. But when you're looking up from a working-class household, made even lower because it's headed by a single mom, everything above you looks like upper class. Everything looked unattainable, closed to me.

Our girls weren't particularly thrilled about going either. Our hosts' children were boys, and everyone knows boys have cooties. But Rachel could tolerate anything if she brought a dozen books and her Barbie dolls. And Cassie was happy to go anywhere that her big sister went, as long as she had her My Little Ponies and Sealie stuffed animal. I wished I had a comfort toy to take along.

For several days, I had hoped for snow, sleet, anything to derail this trip. But, unfortunately, this was a low-snow year and the weather was clear. We were going.

"I'm really looking forward to this," Martin said as he slid behind the wheel. "I haven't seen some of these friends since high school."

I said nothing. I knew he'd take my silence as consent. He always did.

I was happy for him, for his excitement. I wanted him to enjoy our life. He'd left a job he loved for one that was less varied. Medical school was hard on him, as he reminded me often. His hair turned gray from the strain, he claimed.

To be fair, he carried a lot on his broad shoulders. His position at IBM required him to show up each day, think up brilliant computer science-related theorems, collaborate with the other researchers doing the same, and publish results. At home, we shared the child duties: getting kids ready in the morning, taking them to the bus or preschool, relieving the after-school babysitter, making supper, overseeing homework, playing with the girls after supper, bedtime activities, and soothing the girls to sleep. While I did the bulk of cleaning and laundry, he shouldered the not-insignificant "manly" duties such as lawn mowing, toilet plunging, and changing light bulbs.

Martin didn't take time for fun, so how could I begrudge him this two-day retreat to see his childhood buddies?

I didn't bother trying to study on the one-hour trip. First, it felt rude for the front-seat passenger not to engage with the driver. Second, the girls needed frequent attention as their car seats didn't prevent them from reaching over to annoy each other. But between chatting with Martin and chiding the girls, there was plenty of time for me to fret about the upcoming exams.

We drove south to New Jersey while a Raffi cassette of children's songs played. Several queries from the back seat about the likely arrival time punctuated the music. Finally, we pulled up to a stately home in Montclair's historic district. It reminded me of the house I'd worked in as a housekeeper and nanny during college. The house where I could enter only through the rear door and ascend to my maid's quarters via the back stairway. I looked for a path to the back entrance.

At least we'd taken the station wagon, our "upscale" car because it was a Volvo and we'd bought it new. Our other car was a lima-bean green Ford Maverick that squeaked loudly as we drove it at slow speeds. I couldn't drive into a parking lot or down a small street, without people staring at the noisy vehicle. Mechanics had failed to find the cause but pronounced the car safe and sound. But I wasn't safe from the looks on people's faces as they sneered at us lower-class people in their jalopy. Replacing it was off the table at that time—we didn't have the money.

Martin's friends, Bob and Susie, welcomed us warmly and gave us a quick tour of the house. I remember spotless white carpet, at least six bedrooms, and as many bathrooms. Before I could stop her, Rachel opened a built-in cabinet. Stacks of neatly folded plush white towels and linens filled shelves up to the seven-foot ceilings. There wasn't a single raggedy one in the bunch. Our towels were so worn that I had to closely inspect to determine which ones I had already assigned to the rag bag and which were still useable, if not presentable.

The kitchen had two dishwashers. "For entertaining," Susie said when I asked why there were two. Until recently, I'd never even had one dishwasher. I still marveled at the magic of dishes cleaned by the press of a button. I pictured large parties in Susie's house, with women in ball gowns and men in tuxedoes dining on caviar and sipping champagne. In my mind, they mingled in the kitchen, close to the two dishwashers—because that's what fancy rich people must do.

Conversation flowed during dinner; Bob did most of the talking. His enthusiasm was infectious. He loved the steak his wife had prepared. The wine we brought was superb. His boys' football and wrestling teams were all-state champs. I now understood why Martin was so fond of his friend. He made everything fun.

After supper, which ran late, I brought the girls up to bed. They snuggled into a double bed and I lay between them to read a story. I wished I could stay with them, to get some badly needed sleep. My worries about the upcoming exams were not exactly soporific; I'd spent several nights wrinkling the sheets as I tossed around.

Martin's high school crowd began arriving around nine o'clock. They all lived in the tristate area—New Jersey, New York, Connecticut—so they saw each other on occasion. They had not seen Martin in a decade, however. They crowded around him, asking him about his work, his family (not us—his parents and brother), and Seattle. Martin introduced me, but after a quick hello they ignored me. I sat in a chair in a corner while Martin sat across the room, surrounded by his old gang. The distance between my chair and his was probably only eight feet, but it felt like forty. I was the servant in the corner of a ballroom—Martin was on the throne with the lords and ladies.

I carried my impoverished childhood with me into adulthood. As a result, there were many things I didn't know. First, my money knowledge was limited to cash, checks, and my yearly Christmas club savings account. Stocks, bonds, and the myriad other ways rich people invest their money had no meaning for me. People obtained money by working; I didn't realize that money could make money for its owner. I didn't speak business lingo. I'd once asked a CEO's wife what her husband's job title meant. Her eyes wide, it took her several seconds to respond, "He's it. He's at the top." I didn't know how to ski or sail or ride a horse. I tipped coffee shop waitresses—it was easy to calculate the going rate of 15 percent—but how to tip a valet or bellboy flummoxed me. In the movies, the rich guy palmed a bill with a handshake without showing how much money exchanged hands. I never entered a designer clothing store, afraid that my usual method of looking first at the price tag before inspecting an item would not be acceptable. In a jewelry store, I expected to be ignored rather than waited upon.

One woman—tall, slender, single—paid Martin the most attention. Oh, great. How could I compete with an attractive, rich woman whose figure had never been ravaged by pregnancy? A woman whose family had standing box seats at the Metropolitan Opera? A woman whose limousine sat idling outside so it would be warm when she decided to go back to her penthouse in the city?

The hours passed slowly. I snuck looks at my watch every ten minutes. The crowd talked only of high school. Good times. Fun times. I sat watching, wishing I could walk home. I hoped I smiled at their laughter, but I feared my face was morose. Midnight arrived finally. There was champagne, cheering, laughter, hugs all around. Bob and Susie kissed. Martin stayed with his entourage. I don't think he even looked over at me. One a.m. came and went, then 2:00 a.m. I started to feel queasy, the champagne having its own little celebration in my stomach. I wanted to go to bed, to at least catch up on sleep if I couldn't study. But I couldn't leave Martin alone with the temptress. Finally, at 3:00 a.m., she stood up. She looked meaningfully at Martin and told him not to be a stranger. He seemed to remember that I was there, crossed the wide divide between us, and said let's go to bed.

The next morning, we left after a late breakfast. Martin wanted to stop at his mother's apartment in Fort Lee. It was just a few minutes out of the way, but it meant I'd have absolutely no time to study that day. She'd prepared a lunch of cold cuts, old lettuce, and Jell-O and invited as many friends and relatives as she could round up on the holiday. As expected, a dozen of her relatives and friends greeted us as we entered her fourth-floor apartment. All spoke English with the same Austrian-German accent, with frequent German words sprinkled into the conversation. All had brought pastries. The gathering turned from a boring lunch into a typical Austrian coffee and cake afternoon. The girls loved it. Martin loved it. I wanted to leave.

A dozen people asked me how medical school was going. A dozen people asked Martin about his job at IBM. A dozen people asked the girls how they liked living in New York. Feeling like a prisoner, I endured the afternoon. Finally, at four o'clock I stood up and said we had to get home, to give the girls some supper before bedtime.

It had grown dark by the time we got on the road. I turned on the tape deck to Raffi singing that Mama would take us to the zoo tomorrow.

New Jersey thruways and New York parkways rushed past our car like a bad video game. Suddenly, I realized the whooshing wasn't just going on outside the car. It was happening in my head, my arms, my legs. I tingled all over, not in a good way. It was pins and needles, like when you sit on your foot for too long. But this was pins and needles everywhere—face, shoulders, chest, arms, hands, stomach, back, thighs, calves, feet. My heart raced. I was dizzy. I felt short of breath, like my lungs couldn't expand enough to hold the air I needed. My mouth was dry and numb at the same time. I felt nauseous, and yet my throat felt so constricted that I couldn't imagine being able to throw up.

Thinking I might feel better if I couldn't see the rushing traffic, I asked Martin if I could put my head in his lap. I'd never asked to do that in a car before. I'm not sure why I didn't just close my eyes. Perhaps I also wanted the reassurance of touching him. Of course, he said, and kept driving. I was terribly uncomfortable with the stick shift pressing into my chest, my forehead pressing into the steering wheel, my legs bent sideways.

Had I yet studied neurophysiology, I might have realized that I was hyperventilating, which caused me to incompletely release the air I inhaled. This lowered my body's level of carbon dioxide, which can reduce blood calcium levels. I was giving myself a respiratory alkalosis. This may result in dizziness, tingling in the lips, hands or feet, headache, weakness, fainting, and seizures. But we wouldn't complete neurophysiology until the spring. I thought something was terribly wrong but couldn't figure out which body system was primarily responsible. Mostly, I couldn't think. I could only feel these terrible feelings.

The ride home took about sixty minutes, but it felt like sixty hours. Now Raffi was singing about an elephant sitting on him. I felt like an elephant had sat on top of me, smothering me. I managed to answer the girls' inevitable questions about when we would arrive home. At least whatever was happening in my brain hadn't affected my speech.

Suddenly Rachel said, "I feel sick." We swung into action. Martin looked for a thruway exit. I told Rachel to roll down her window (our old Volvo had only manual window controls). I sat up, feeling vertigo in a way I knew was me, not the world. I prayed that Rachel wouldn't spew. I wasn't sure I could move my limbs to clean her up. Cassie announced that she was sick, too.

I turned on the car dome light. Rachel looked her usual car-sick green. I grabbed one of the plastic vegetable bags we recycled into the glove compartment for this purpose. I hoped it hadn't held carrots. We'd learned the hard way that carrots dug holes in the bottom of plastic bags—not good for containing throw-up. By now, Martin had steered us onto a little suburban road. He pulled over, got Rachel out of the car for some anti-nausea breaths of air, and we waited for her stomach to calm down. Cassie fussed that she wanted to get out of the car, so I distracted her with My Little Ponies. Through all this, I noticed that my pins and needles had subsided, although my hands were still trembling, and my own stomach was acting up. But something had improved, and I had no idea why. Rachel announced she felt better, we got her settled back in her seat, and we made the rest of the journey home.

I studied for an hour that night. I hoped it would buy me passing grades in the upcoming exams, but I feared the worst.

Chapter 10

JANUARY 1986

Four days after the exams, our grades were posted on the corkboard outside the anatomy labs. Ten pages of eight-by-eleven-inch computer paper, each with twenty numbers corresponding to student IDs and grades for the three exams. My number was hidden by the taller students in front of me, so I had to wait until they found their grades. One by one they said, "Yes," whooped a little, and moved out of the way. Heart pounding, I found my number. My heart sped even faster when I saw that two of my three grades were below the passing cut-point of 70 percent. In shock, I bowed my head, retreated from the crowd, and ran to the ladies' room. There, I tried to slow my breathing, tried to think.

These were the first exams I'd ever failed. In my entire life. Except that one history test in sophomore year of high school when I didn't realize we had to memorize the actual numbers of the Articles of the US Constitution. Well, there was that one college calculus test that I'd taken during a term in which I'd fallen in love and couldn't concentrate on math. (Luckily, my love—now my husband—was an applied math major. He told me I just needed to concentrate, and then tutored me so well that I aced my final exam.) And there was the organic chemistry test I'd taken in graduate school when I couldn't remember the standard numbering system for sugar molecules.

Failing these exams now threatened to derail my dreams of becoming a doctor. The results put me into an immediate panic. I'd flunk out of school. It would prove that I wasn't worthy of being a doctor. I just wasn't smart enough.

I'd have to tell Martin and the girls that their sacrifices had been a waste. We'd have to reevaluate our life plans. I'd need to look for work. My skills were academic. Even if I could land a job in one of the New York City universities with epidemiology programs, I'd have a horrendous commute to and from Yorktown Heights every day. But, since Martin's move to IBM was supposed to be a temporary situation while I went to medical school, he'd most likely want to look for a university teaching and research position. The chance of both of us landing academic jobs in the same city would be minimal.

Then there would be the shame. Our relatives would know that I wasn't worthy. Martin's family were all brilliant, studious types. I felt like a stupid peasant in comparison. Now it was clear that I really was a stupid peasant. My mother would say I shouldn't have tried to do something above myself. That I was too big for my britches. She would be right.

I had more immediate worries. The grades list said to contact my professors for remedial plans. I'd have to meet with them in person. There would no longer be the large, impersonal distance between the podium and my seat at the back of the lecture hall. I'd have to talk face-to-face with a professor who wouldn't think very much of the flunky in front of him.

In most of my academic career, I'd been a back-of-the-auditorium type of student. I feared the professors, as if they were deities to my mere mortal-ness. In the medical school classroom that sloped down to the professor's lectern, I routinely chose a top row seat on the far-right aisle, as close as possible to the exit—in case I needed a quick escape. I was an anonymous body in my classes. I assumed the teachers—the exalted males—would have no interest in such a lowly creature as myself. I was in their class but not in their Class.

I saw other students talk with their professors, go to their office hours, become known. I thought of them as suck-ups, currying favor, grubbing for grades. But I envied the ease with which they did this, the comfort they seemed to have with the professors. I'd been able to experience a little of this in my PhD program, but only because it's impossible to earn a PhD without interacting with at least one professor. I didn't get close to all my teachers, but I met weekly with my PhD advisor. This one-on-one mentorship benefitted me greatly as a PhD graduate student, but here in medical school, I practiced my usual prof-avoidance. In my mind, I had no right to approach a teacher individually.

Years before, my college Intro to Psychology professor said that girls who succeed largely do so because of having a strong relationship with their father. That perspective had always bothered me. I'd grown up without a father and felt the lack daily, although I thought I'd done well academically despite not having a dad. I was mostly an A-student in school and graduated from college and graduate school. But, looking back, I can see how girls and women who were comfortable with men could excel in an academic venue. The female students who were able to see professors as caring father figures would be more comfortable asking for help. They could approach the University Dad with the same confidence they approached Home Dad. Of course, University Dad would be happy to stop everything and help the little girl in need—because that's what dads do.

Over the years, I've seen this comfort with father figures help women succeed in academic careers. Many women who hold positions of power began their careers under the tutelage of a senior male mentor. Often, these women provide years of assistance to the men, running their studies and doing other work to promote the man's prominence. In return, when the men were close to retirement, they conferred positions of power and prestige on the women. It's more *Suck Up* than *Lean In*.

While I'd been married since the age of twenty-three and with my husband for four years before that, I didn't really understand men. I didn't know how to be a daughter-figure. I didn't know how to ask a man for help. Instead, I assumed no man would want to help me and that if I asked a man to do anything, he'd dismiss me. Perhaps I'd even anger him by my request, and he'd punish me for daring to ask him to do something for me.

Now, I had no choice but to meet my professors. The first—the biochemist—had a tiny, crowded office at the bottom floor of a dingy building. Maybe this professor wasn't so exalted after all. My heart pounded throughout the entire ten-minute conversation. I expected him to tell me I was too stupid to pass his class. Instead, he asked me if I'd passed my other tests. I told him about the physiology exam.

"Is there anything going on in your life now? Any problems at home?"

This shocked me. Why was he interested in my private life? I didn't know what to say. How could I tell him about my recent breast cancer scare, my mother and aunt's strained visit, my two kids who clamored for my attention, a husband who didn't love me, and the nightly attacks that paralyzed me with terror?

"No," I said. I felt my cheeks burn.

He gave me some printed materials and said gently that I should learn them for the makeup test. I took the papers without looking at them, thanked him, and left.

The meeting with the physiology teacher went similarly. His office was bigger and on a top floor. *He must have a higher status*, I thought. I left the physiology prof's office with a similar set of papers and instructions to memorize all.

Both makeup exams would be in two weeks. However, I still had to keep up with the ongoing classes. There'd be no slack cut for me, no extra time to study for the regularly scheduled tests. Clearly, I couldn't fail any additional exams—there just would not be enough time to keep up with ongoing material as well as make up for failures.

Two weeks later, the girls were finally asleep. I sat on my bed surrounded by textbooks and papers. The makeup material turned out to be several double-sided, single-spaced pages of small-print typing. *Learn this!* Which meant, *memorize this!* Martin came into the room and began to get ready for bed. I looked at the clock—11:00 p.m.—I needed to get to sleep, too. Our days began early with school and work and kids. But I didn't yet feel prepared for the next day's tests. I wanted to ask Martin to quiz me on the memorized material, but I didn't want to keep him up. So, I said nothing, cleared my books and papers, stacked them on my night table that looked like it could topple over with its burdens, and got ready for bed.

I lay beside Martin while he read a novel. I thought about the exams. The two professors were very accommodating of my schedule. I'd take one exam in the lunch break and one after the last class. I thought about the current material I needed to learn for the regular exams coming in two weeks. I thought about my hopes of becoming a doctor. I thought about how hard it all was, much harder than I had expected.

Suddenly, I felt a tingling in my left leg. Oh God, I thought, I'm having a stroke. Then I noticed it in my right leg also. Both of my legs were tingling, like the pins-and-needles feeling you get in your foot from sitting the wrong way. But I wasn't putting undue pressure on either leg. I was just lying in my comfortable bed beside my husband. My hands soon grew numb, then the back of my head, and then my entire head.

My heart pounded. I couldn't breathe. My hearing worked—no problem hearing Martin turning pages in his book. I was having another attack. I turned to Martin.

"Huh?" he mumbled.

"It's happening again. I'm numb all over."

"What's happening again?"

I hadn't yet told him about these attacks. It was an unfortunate moment to tell him for the first time.

"I'm numb all over. I can't breathe."

He sat up, put his book down, and looked at me.

"I think I need a doctor," I said.

"What do you want to do?" he asked.

"I don't know. Maybe I need an ambulance."

"Really?"

"What can I do?"

"Why don't you call our doctor's office? His service will answer."

"Can you call for me?"

He dialed the number and talked with someone. Then he handed me the phone. An answering service operator asked me questions. I told her my symptoms. She said she'd have the doctor call me back. Martin and I got back into bed. He lay on his back, looking at the ceiling. I lay on my side, looking at him, watching him breathe. I still felt numb, but it felt good to watch his chest move up and down. Fifteen minutes later the phone rang. Martin answered it quickly. He didn't want the phone to wake the girls, I realized. He handed me the receiver.

"This is Dr. Stevens. My service said your heart is racing?" I recognized the voice of our internist, who had a solo practice in the town next to ours. His voice was clear, not at all sleepy, quite surprising for midnight.

"Yes, my heart is racing. And I'm feeling numb all over. Like pins and needles."

"How fast is your heart going? Take your pulse."

"One hundred and twenty," I replied a half-minute later. Normal is sixty to one hundred beats per minute. My heart rate was high but not dangerous.

He asked about my other symptoms. Then he asked how much coffee I'd had to drink that day. His voice seemed rushed now, like he didn't want to dawdle.

Mentally I added up the two cups to get me going in the morning, the mega-coffee-to-go from the 7-Eleven after I'd dropped Cassie at her preschool, the tasteless super-size coffees from the medical school's cafeteria at lunchtime and again before it closed at 2:00 p.m.

"About seven or eight cups." I didn't mention the nonstop cups of tea I'd had from four o'clock on. He hadn't asked about tea.

"It's all that coffee. I was once hospitalized with heart palpitations from coffee," he said. "It took days for my heart rate to normalize." His voice grew louder and sped up even more as he talked.

"But what do I do tonight?"

"Drink a lot of water," he said. Then he paused, and as if finally realizing that there might be something other than coffee-overload going on, continued at a slower pace, "Take some deep breaths. Get some sleep and call me tomorrow if your heart is still racing." He hung up.

I looked over at the bed. Martin was asleep. I drank two large glasses of water, knowing they'd wake my bladder in a couple of hours. I lay down and thought. I hoped the doctor was right—I would gladly eliminate coffee if that did away with these attacks.

It didn't. Despite replacing my coffee habit with decaf, every few nights I'd find myself fearful, sweating, gasping for breath, and numb all over.

I began to think I was losing my mind. Growing up in Boston in the '50s and '60s, I learned that people with psychiatric issues were called "crazy," or worse, put into insane asylums and left there to rot. In working-class Boston, no one went to a therapist. If you needed advice on a life matter, including marriage, you went to your parish priest—the least experienced person possible. But you would never visit a psychiatrist or a psychologist. To see a doctor that specializes in the mind meant that you were losing your mind.

I was petrified at the thought of being locked up in an institution. I was convinced that if anyone knew about my symptoms, I'd be shut up in a mental hospital, never to see my girls again. They'd grow up without a mother.

A week after the makeups, I found two white envelopes in my school mailbox. Epinephrine flooded my entire circulatory system and my hands shook so hard I had difficulty opening the mail. They were my makeup exam results—I'd passed both tests. Relief flooded my body, mixing with the epinephrine. I allowed myself ten seconds of self-congratulations, and then remembered the next set of exams coming and how I was in high danger of failing again.

By now, we'd begun our next block of first-year courses. There was Neuroanatomy, the study of the brain and nervous system structures. Then there was Behavioral Medicine, an introduction to psychiatry and the relationships between the mind and health. In a third course, Neurophysiology, we studied the science of how our central and peripheral nervous systems control all that we do. Finally, we continued with our Clinical Medicine course. For the next few months, we'd focus on the brain at the same time that my own brain failed me.

My mother and stepfather liked to steam lobsters in the summer. My stepfather would buy the lobsters off a trawler as soon as it pulled into Plymouth Harbor. He'd rush them home in big plastic bags and lower them head first into the large pot of boiling water my mother had ready on the stove. That way they don't feel any pain, he told me. I was skeptical; if the creatures felt no pain, why did they wriggle so much as my stepfather lowered them into the steam? I felt like medical school had dropped me head first into a cauldron with the massive amount of material churning like boiling water. The posture did nothing to lessen the scalding pain.

In the middle of neuroanatomy class, an attack snuck up on me. The professor had just described the following week's practical exam. Sections of brain specimens would be laid out on lab tables. We'd have to identify each accurately. There would be no multiple-choice options, nothing to jog your memory. You either knew it or you didn't. I imagined my brain cut up into pieces. The section of my brain responsible for memorizing thousands of anatomical structures and physiological facts must be minuscule, I thought. I *had* to pass all my upcoming classes. It wasn't clear if the school would allow me to repeatedly fail and make up exams.

The pins and needles feeling started in my fingers this time and spread up my arms. Then, I felt the sensation around my mouth and cheeks. My calves grew numb all over, followed by my thighs. I sat frozen, afraid a scream would escape from my mouth, that I'd have no control over my voice or the rest of my body. My heart pounded; I was too petrified to count my pulse. It felt as though I was running for my life, trying to escape an unspeakable evil. I pictured someone calling the medics who would strap me onto a stretcher and take me to the psychiatric wing of the hospital. They'd lock me away forever.

Unable to tolerate sitting in that room surrounded by strangers, I rose and fled. I sped to the ladies' room and splashed water on my face. I wasn't sure why I did this, but I'd seen it work for women in distress in the movies. Of course, their distress might be because their love interest flirted with someone else at a bar. Or perhaps they were forced to wear ugly bridesmaid dresses. Not one of them was facing failure at medical school while raising children.

The splashed water didn't help, just soaked my sweater and shirt. I hurried out to my car, the frigid February air on my wet upper body barely registering. Maybe if I left the scene of the attack, I'd feel better. Some sane thoughts filtered through my panic. Most importantly, I realized that the panic attacks would not go away by themselves. They were here to stay, unless I did something about them. Since nothing I'd done had helped—ignoring them, drinking alcohol, pretending they only occurred at home at night—I needed expert advice. I rummaged through the notebooks strewn on the passenger seat and found the one I'd used on my first day of medical school orientation. The one in which I had written down the number of the medical school psychiatrist who said to call him when we eventually needed help.

I needed help.

Chapter 11

JANUARY 1986

I dialed the number the psychiatrist had written on the blackboard the last day of orientation week. The number I'd thought I'd never need. Not wanting anyone at school to overhear my phone conversation, I called from a gas station a mile from the medical school. My hand shook so much I had trouble punching the payphone buttons. I could see my breath in the phone booth's frigid air. I hoped I'd reach the psychiatrist, he'd tell me to come right in to see him, I'd have a diagnosis and a cure that afternoon, and be in Yorktown Heights by two o'clock in time to pick up Cassie at preschool and meet Rachel at her bus. I liked to plan out my days.

Unfortunately, things didn't work out that way. His secretary answered and said, "No he's not here. Can I take a message?"

"But how can I reach him?"

If my voice sounded panicky, it didn't seem to bother her. Maybe she was used to people calling her boss in a panic.

"If you leave a message, he'll call you back."

Reluctantly, I left my home number, the only number I could give in the days before cell phones. I wasn't sure that I wanted my husband to know I had called a shrink. I certainly didn't want my mother-in-law, who was babysitting the next afternoon, to know, and I didn't want to burden the girls with the knowledge that their mother was going insane. As if I could hide crazy, like covering up a suspicious mole.

Dr. Jones called back shortly after I arrived home at one o'clock. He didn't offer to see me that day or the next. Instead, he asked me where I lived. I thought he was going to suggest a home visit and was about to protest. But when I told him I lived in Yorktown Heights, he gave me the names of two psychiatrists and their phone numbers. He said both were excellent, practiced near where I lived, and would take good care of me. I liked that last part. After we hung up, I looked at the two names—one woman, one man. I rejected the woman immediately. I couldn't imagine a female doctor being sympathetic. The irony of this escaped me—here I was trying to become a female doctor. I chose the man. His name was Dr. Jack Shapiro.

Dr. Shapiro's voicemail instructed me to leave my name and number, and if it was an emergency to call 911 or the mental health hotline. While I did feel like I was having an emergency, I didn't quite know how to word it. It wasn't like I'd just cut myself and had arterial blood pumping out of an open wound. I wasn't about to give birth. I could barely describe my symptoms to myself, let alone someone over the phone. I left my name and number, and said I was feeling anxious. I worried that I'd miss his return call. But I had to pick up the girls, so just hoped he'd leave a message on our home answering machine.

I felt better as soon I walked into Cassie's preschool. Her classroom was alive with little girls and boys who giggled and jumped and danced as they waited for their moms to pick them up. We met Rachel at her school bus stop and came home.

The phone was ringing as we walked into the house at three o'clock. The girls dashed to be first to answer it. Cassie won, and she announced, "It's some guy for you, Mom."

It was Dr. Shapiro. He asked me if I could come in that afternoon at four o'clock. Yes, I could, I said, hoping the teenager down the street could babysit until 5:15 when Martin arrived home. I felt so relieved—this doctor would figure out my problem, give me some pills, and I'd be back to normal and able to get on with school and home life.

Luckily, the teenager down the street was free. The girls didn't mind at all that Mom would be going out. This neighbor was the girls' favorite babysitter because she entertained them for hours with stories. I called Martin and simply told him I'd made an appointment to see a psychiatrist that afternoon for my attacks. He said it sounded like a good idea and not to worry—he'd take care of supper.

Everything was going smoothly. So why was my stomach churning?

Over the next half hour, I was too busy with the girls to fret about the upcoming appointment. They needed Mom to make them a snack and to help them find favorite toys. They needed me to referee a disagreement about who owned the most My Little Ponies. Cassie fell and required an emergency bandage and hug.

The babysitter arrived on time, I kissed the girls, and drove the couple of miles to my appointment. On the way, I rehearsed what I'd say to the psychiatrist. I'd make sure to tell him that I wasn't a lunatic. I'd reassure him that I didn't want to kill myself. I'd tell him I was just nervous. I had decided that I suffered from an Anxiety Disorder. While I was okay with saying I felt anxious because it was what it was, I wasn't keen on the idea of having a *disorder*. But that's how psychiatrists seemed to classify some psychological issues—a disorder, as if it were the opposite of order. Something not neat. I had to admit that my mind was anything but neat. At any one moment I had so many thoughts running through my head that it got quite messy in there.

I'd come to my self-diagnosed condition from our Behavioral Medicine course. Fascinated by the topic because it was about patients instead of brains and bones and biochemistry, I devoured the assigned textbook sections. I read about all the psychiatric disorders, in part to see if I had any of them. First were the psychotic disorders. I was relieved to note that, no, I wasn't having any auditory hallucinations—there were no voices in my head. Next came the mood disorders. I did sometimes feel down but didn't fit the criteria for major depression or for bipolar disease. I didn't have a factitious disorder; I wasn't making up signs and symptoms of illness, although I wasn't sure if my catastrophizing every small illness could count for a touch of this disorder. I didn't currently have an eating disorder, unless chocolate addiction counted. I wasn't suffering from substance abuse, not really, unless the several drinks I had on the night after exam periods were excessive enough to call it a disorder.

There were personality disorders, so many that I couldn't keep them straight: paranoid, schizoid, schizotypal, antisocial, borderline, histrionic, narcissistic, avoidant, dependent, and obsessive-compulsive. There was also a catch-all personality disorder not otherwise specified, I guessed this was for cases in which a doctor couldn't figure out in which category a patient belonged. I had a lot of the traits listed in several of these personality disorders, particularly avoidant and dependent ones, and maybe a little bit of paranoid.

I came upon the anxiety disorder chapter and felt like the authors were describing me. I learned that there were several major types of this illness. I had some aspects of all of them. There was Generalized Anxiety Disorder, characterized by chronic anxiety and exaggerated worry and tension, even when there is little or nothing to provoke it. This described me well, worried about everything, although I was not happy with the specification that there was nothing to provoke it. There were a lot of scary things in the world—how could these authors think there was little or nothing to provoke my worries?

Next came Obsessive-Compulsive Disorder, OCD, in which a person has recurrent, unwanted thoughts (obsessions) and/or repetitive behaviors (compulsions). Would my constant thoughts of flunking out of medical school qualify? The repetitive behaviors such as hand washing, counting, checking, or cleaning are often performed with the hope of preventing obsessive thoughts or making them go away. I did wash my hands a lot, especially when under stress, such as when my relatives or in-laws visited.

There were the phobic disorders, subdivided into Agoraphobia, with or without panic attacks, Social Phobia, and Simple Phobia. *Hmmm*, I thought. I did get very nervous at parties. Could that mean I had Agoraphobia? And I had aversions to several things like bobby pins, rubber bands, and bees. I'd avoid touching bobby pins and rubber bands, and I avoided eating items outdoors that attracted bees.

Another illness—Panic Disorder—caused unexpected and repeated episodes of intense fear accompanied by physical symptoms that could include chest pain, heart palpitations, shortness of breath, dizziness, or abdominal distress. My attacks did have several of these symptoms. The chapter didn't mention the full-body pins-and-needles feeling, however.

Then came Social Phobia, or Social Anxiety Disorder, which is characterized by overwhelming anxiety and excessive self-consciousness in everyday social situations. In severe forms, individuals may experience symptoms anytime they are around other people. I definitely had some of this, I decided.

Finally came Post-Traumatic Stress Disorder, PTSD, an anxiety disorder that can develop after exposure to a terrifying event or ordeal in which grave physical harm occurred or was threatened. I couldn't say that medical school was a terrifying event, although it petrified me. I didn't yet realize that the events of my childhood would qualify as terrifying.

This new knowledge led me to think I was dealing with anxiety. I still didn't know what precipitated the attacks, but I knew I felt anxious about

100 percent of the time. Even more reassuring was the text's information on available treatments. That's it, I decided. I just needed some pills.

Looking back, I can see that I also showed signs of the *medical student's syndrome*, which happens when doctors-in-training decide that they have contracted an illness they are learning about. I didn't know this syndrome existed, nor did I think that other students might be diagnosing themselves from our readings. Still, the readings helped me realize that what I may have been dealing with could be treated.

I realized I'd been anxious all my life. A racing heart, sweaty palms, shaking, twisting stomach—these were all frequent experiences. It wouldn't take much to set them off. Public speaking was one but not just presenting to an audience. I'd get nervous just talking to a shop clerk, making a phone call to someone I didn't know, stopping to ask for directions. I'd panic when alone in my house. When Martin traveled on a business trip, all house sounds were someone trying to break in. I feared conflict, afraid to contradict my husband or anyone else. I hated hearing a child reprimanded, which is kind of a difficult thing to avoid when living with small children. I dreaded illness. Every sniffle, ache, or odd sensation grew in my mind to a terminal illness. I thought I'd succumb and leave my babies without a mommy.

Many of these fears began in childhood. A latchkey kid, I'd check for bogeymen under each bed and in every closet on arriving home after school. I feared the wrath of my mother, teachers, nuns, priests, men, God, and other kids, not necessarily in that order. The fight-or-flight symptoms—heart racing, abdominal distress—occurred daily, fifteen minutes before my mother arrived home. I knew that if I hadn't completed my chores, she'd give me a slapping. Another continuous worry was that my mother would make good on her frequent threats to send me away—to an institution, to another home, to my father, wherever she could dump me. I worried that my Aunt Margie, who lived with us, would someday leave. Whenever she and my mother fought, which was frequently, she'd threaten to move out. I worried that I was so much of a sinner for secretly hating my mother that God would smite me dead.

Beginning in second grade, I had severe school anxiety. We'd moved to a new apartment, away from the neighbor girls I walked to school with and played with after school. I'd lost my little tribe. In the new apartment, I'd get ready each morning in slow-motion time. I poured my Alpha-Bits cereal, watched the letters float in the milk, spelled out words, and ate the letters one at a time. All the while, I wished that it wasn't a school day, that I wasn't so fat, and that I had friends at school. I'd hope the nun wouldn't call on me and that the kids wouldn't call me fatso in the playground.

It never occurred to me to tell my mother that I was afraid to go to school. She didn't want to see or hear from me in the mornings. My view of her was the back page of the *Boston Globe* she held in front of her while sitting at the kitchen table. Beside her, a cup of black coffee grew cold and a Tareyton cigarette smoldered. If I dawdled too long, she'd bark a command to hurry up for school.

As I pulled into the doctor's parking lot, I decided I wouldn't go into my childhood anxieties. I just wanted a speedy diagnosis and a quick cure.

Chapter 12

JANUARY 1986

I climbed out of my car and stood outside a two-story, dark brown, Victorian house. I thought I must have the wrong place because this did not look like a doctor's office. But the address was correct, and I saw a little sign pointing to the back yard that said, "Dr. Jack Shapiro." An icy path led behind the house, and a door opened to rickety stairs leading up to the second floor. Convinced that I would be barging in on someone's private home, I wasn't sure whether my anxiety would be exacerbated or cured that day.

I had never seen any type of therapist. My only counseling experience had been the twenty-minute premarital meeting Martin and I had with the Catholic priest who would marry us. We'd decided on a Catholic church wedding to appease my relatives. I thought that some would not attend a secular wedding. In retrospect, that would have been okay.

It was the '70s, and the priest was a fellow sociology graduate student. Not quite a hippy but cool enough. That he agreed to marry a lapsed Catholic and an avowed atheist described him and the era. During the premarital counseling session, he told us the Church rules on marriage and childrearing without asking us if we would abide by them. He knew the answer—that we had no intention of practicing the religion or of raising our eventual children as Catholic. He seemed okay with what we'd say but didn't want to lie to the Church when he signed our marriage certificate.

I'd once had a disastrous date with a psychologist-in-training. He had practiced "thank you for sharing that with me" so many times it made me want to kick him out the door to see if he thanked me for that. We had just the one date.

At the top of the stairs was a waiting area with two well-worn folding chairs. The space was so tiny that a patient leaving the doctor's office would have to crawl over the knees of anyone sitting there. A closed door had a small "Jack Shapiro, MD" nameplate. I wondered where the receptionist sat. At 4:00 p.m. exactly, the door opened. A tall, thin, man in his late thirties or early forties with a premature stoop leaned his head out and smiled under his bushy red-brown mustache.

"Anne?" he asked.

"Yes," I said.

"Come in."

I walked in, surprised to find myself in a cross between a living room and an office, about ten feet wide by eight feet deep. The furniture looked like it had been found curbside on garbage pick-up day. There was a small rickety desk. The lack of a receptionist surprised me; I thought all physicians had support people to help them do their doctoring stuff.

Dr. Shapiro pointed to a chair and a sofa. "Sit where you'd like," he said.

I didn't see myself lying on the maroon horse-hair couch telling my inner secrets to this stranger. I chose the small, dusky-blue chair with padded arms and seat; I thought I could hold myself together in it. A box of tissues sat on the small round table next to my chair. How considerate that the doctor would make sure a patient with a cold would be comfortable. It didn't occur to me that people cried in psychiatrists' offices.

The doctor sat across from me in a shabby, high-backed brown upholstered chair, one leg crossed over the other. He wore blue jeans, a plaid flannel shirt, and brown suede Hush Puppies. *What kind of doctor wears blue jeans to see patients*, I wondered? He set a pad of yellow-lined paper on his lap and clicked open a pen.

"You can call me Jack," he said.

I said nothing, taken aback at the idea of addressing a doctor by his given name. How could a doctor, a human god, go by his first name, especially to me, a lowly female patient?

"Okay," he said. "Why don't you tell me what's been going on."

"I've been having these nervous attacks." My parched throat had a hard time letting the words out. He leaned forward to hear me.

"What do they feel like?" he asked.

I pulled at a strand of my hair. I worried that the sweat pouring from my armpits would show on my sweater.

"Well, I feel very scared and my heart races and my legs go numb and I feel like I'm going to pass out."

"I see. How long do they last?"

"At least a half hour. Sometimes hours. They usually happen at night, in bed, and then I can't sleep at all."

"Do they come on suddenly, or do you feel anxious ahead of time?"

"I don't know."

"Well, can you remember what you were thinking or feeling before they start?"

I hesitated, felt my cheeks getting hot.

"I don't like talking about my feelings," I said.

"You're going to have to get over that," he said. "I'm big into feelings."

I didn't say anything. I thought psychiatrists were supposed to be understanding. This guy was cruel, telling me already to get over something.

"Let me ask you some things about yourself. Have you been feeling sad lately?"

"Not particularly."

"What kinds of things do you do for fun?"

"Hanging out with my family. My husband and I have two daughters."

"How old are they?"

"Seven and almost four."

"What are their names?"

"Rachel and Cassie."

"What sorts of things do you do with them that you enjoy?"

"Anything. I enjoy playing with them at home. They love playing with Barbies and My Little Ponies. They like to bring all the blankets and pillows in the house into the living room and pretend there's a grand adventure with oceans and monsters. I like to read to them—we bring armloads of books home from the library every week. And I like taking them to a park and to their lessons."

He smiled as I talked. "How's your sleep been?"

"Not great. I lie in bed for hours worrying about things. I can't fall asleep."

"Have you ever thought about hurting yourself?"

"Oh God no." I figured he meant suicide. The last thing I'd want would be to leave my girls motherless. I'd never even considered it. Years later I'd learn that suicide among medical students and physicians was a thing. The rates of attempted and completed suicides in these trainees and professionals far exceed that in the general United States population. At the time, no one talked about mental illness, stress, and other things that can lead to these tragic events. Doctors had to be virile, impervious to the strains of job and life, able to withstand excessive work demands, insufficient sleep, and the emotional toil of dealing daily with life and death situations.

Jack asked more about my life. He learned we'd just moved to Yorktown Heights the previous summer and that I was a first-year medical student. He raised an eyebrow.

On his prodding, I went into detail about when Martin and I married and our family history in Seattle and move to New York. Yes, both girls were happy and healthy, doing well at school (Rachel in second grade in public school, Cassie in Montessori preschool). Yes, Martin was a successful computer scientist at IBM Research and seemed happy.

"Tell me about your childhood."

I grew impatient. I still had no diagnosis, and he had yet to mention treatment. On his prompting, I gave him an abbreviated version of my Irish-Catholic childhood in Boston. My parents separated before I was born, my mother farmed me out to other homes and a Catholic boarding school until I was five years old. I came home only on weekends. After that, I lived with my mother and aunt. My mother was a secretary and my aunt worked as a file clerk. I didn't meet my father until I was sixteen years old. He rarely paid child support. Really, I didn't see what all this had to do with my current craziness.

"Did you love your mother?"

"No, I hated her." The words surprised me—I'd never uttered them to anyone before.

"Why?"

I tried to swallow. I strained to make my voice work.

"She hit me a lot. She screamed at me. Sometimes she stopped talking to me for days or weeks at a time. And she threatened to kick me out." Damn, I usually kept this all secret, but this guy had a way of pulling things out of me.

My heart pounded. I waited for him to tell me I was lying. I'd never told anyone these things about my mother, assuming people wouldn't believe me. I'd not even told my husband. My aunt had witnessed the treatment but had done nothing to intervene.

I began to wonder if this man was an imposter. I'd heard about patients killing their psychiatrists. Maybe an insane patient had broken into

Dr. Shapiro's office right before me, murdered the shrink, hid his body, and now was pretending to be my doctor.

I crossed and uncrossed my legs but still felt unsettled. I never talked about myself, not to anyone. Oh, I could tell Martin that I loved chocolate and hated licorice. I felt comfortable telling him I was freezing as I shoved the thermostat up to seventy-five degrees. I told the girls that burping loudly on purpose was unacceptable for young ladies (they didn't listen). But I never talked about how I felt about anything. The quiet one in any gathering, I listened intently to what others said, but I rarely contributed.

It wasn't that I was purposefully secretive. I just couldn't believe that people would want to know anything about me. In a group, especially of women, I never knew how to make my voice heard through the flow of conversation. I didn't have the "gift of gab," unlike many of my relatives and friends of Irish decent.

"Did your mother ever have psychiatric treatment?"

"No."

"Did any of your relatives drink to excess?"

"My mother and aunt didn't drink. There was almost never any liquor in the house. Their father was an alcoholic and my father also. I think these men's drinking led my mother and aunt to avoid alcohol. Also, liquor was too expensive for us." I paused. "We were poor," I added quietly, ashamed of this fact as always.

"Tell me about your aunt. What was her name?"

"Margie. She was nicer. She didn't hit me. She was nuts, though."

"How so?"

"She hated men, and she was just odd. She was afraid of a lot of things— heights, thunderstorms, knives, horses. She couldn't throw anything away, and she took a lot of time doing things like washing dishes or leaving the apartment. She had to keep checking that lights were off, the door was locked, and the stove was off."

"Did your mother or aunt have trouble with anxiety or depression?"

I thought hard about this. We didn't use those words when I was a child. Someone might have a "nervous breakdown" or "have a case of the nerves." But it wasn't necessarily considered a condition or disorder.

"My mother seemed histrionic at times. She cried and yelled a lot. Once when she was driving, she became so upset that she pulled off the road to vomit. When she was in her fifties, her doctor gave her a prescription for Valium. So maybe she was anxious, but maybe everyone had Valium then. My aunt used to have what she called "nervous" times. She'd sit at the kitchen table, with a washcloth to her forehead, for hours without moving."

"How about your father? Sometimes anxiety disorders can be inherited."

"I never talked with him until he was in his late forties, and he was usually drunk when I saw him. One time he called me in a panic about something, but his words were slurred so I knew he'd been drinking. He also took a lot of Valium."

The psychiatrist asked if I had any current medical illnesses. I said no, other than the recent breast biopsy. He asked more questions about my school experiences in childhood and my time in university. He asked about drinking and illicit drugs. I responded that I drank a little too much when I'd finished a set of exams but only after the girls had gone to bed. I added that I couldn't drink other nights because I always needed to study. He asked what "a little too much" meant. About three glasses of wine, I said. I told him I'd tried pot in college, but it had made me feel paranoid. I didn't bother to tell him about the one "downer" pill I'd bought for a dollar from a girl down the hall in my college dorm that just made me sleepy. I also didn't mention the time I'd taken an "upper" in college to study for a test. It kept me delightfully awake all night while I studied diligently. At four o'clock in the morning I'd discovered I'd studied the wrong material.

"Well, our time is almost up today," Jack said. "I'm going to give you some numbers. You've been having panic attacks, and we need to figure out what is causing them in order to help you stop having them. If you have a panic attack, you can call my answering service. I check messages several times a day and evening and will call you back. If you don't hear from me soon and feel like it's an emergency, you can call this hotline. The phone counselors there are very helpful for patients in crisis. I work there part-time also."

I took the piece of paper from him. I wanted to ask him exactly what panic attacks were and what caused them. But I was too eager to get out of there.

"I'm also going to give you a prescription for some medication that can help calm you down when you're having a panic attack. It's lorazepam. I'm giving you a prescription for ten pills, for the lowest dose available. Take one if you are having an attack. Don't take it with alcohol, and don't drive for several hours after you've taken it. It can make you sleepy, but since your panic attacks are mostly at night, that would be a good thing."

"Thanks." I took the prescription.

"Let's make some more appointments. I'll need to see you twice a week."

I felt crushed. The doctor hadn't given me a firm diagnosis other than to say I was having panic attacks; but, if I had to come see him twice a week, he must have thought I was completely psycho. So, I really was going insane. I'd better agree to those appointments or else he might commit me to a mental hospital. Not to see my girls would be worse than a death sentence. I arranged twice-weekly regular appointments and left on wobbly legs. Those appointments would take away some of my few precious study hours.

On the way home, I worried about how I would break the news to my husband that his wife was completely bonkers.

꩜

I arrived home to the smells of Martin's Viennese fried chicken cooking and the sounds of the girls playing. Before my coat was off, Rachel appeared at the top of the stairs.

"Mom make her stop," she pleaded. Her tormentor appeared beside her grinning.

"What's going on?" I asked.

"She keeps taking my Barbie doll."

"But I need to play Barbie, too!" Cassie retorted.

I played go-between for a couple of minutes, then left the girls to sort it out in their room. For once, I didn't have to yell, "No hitting!" because these Barbie negotiations were verbal.

I started toward the kitchen to kiss Martin hello.

"Supper's almost ready," he announced to me and anyone else in earshot. Not that the girls would pay any attention until we'd called them at least three times.

Supper was unusually calm and relaxing. I even ate seconds, which was rare for me because my stomach usually twisted in knots with any family conflict. I supervised the girls' bath, we got them ready for bed, and Martin read them a chapter from *Alice in Wonderland* while I cleaned up from supper.

After I loaded the dishwasher, I noticed the floor was covered with so much detritus that it looked like a chicken yard at feeding time. I took the broom from a closet and began to sweep. I always noticed dirt on floors. As a child, I'd receive a beating if I hadn't done my chores before my mother arrived home. I'd learned to notice floors, to make a quick judgment of how likely my mother was to notice that I'd forgotten to sweep.

As I moved the broom back and forth in small arcs that night, I kept my head down, not able to look up at the beauty around me—my family, my home, the honor of being in medical school, the promise of entering a prestigious profession. I could only focus on the mucky exams and my messy mind.

Chapter 13

I slid past Jack into his office and sat in the chair opposite his. The room smelled of dust. I sat bolt upright, knees locked, hands clenched, locking in every feeling as if I even knew when and what feelings I had. It was my second session, three days after the first.

"How are you doing?" he asked.

"Okay." I bit my inner lip.

"Have you had any panic attacks since our last session?"

"Yes, last night."

"Did you try the lorazepam?"

"No." I waited to be scolded. Jack didn't press the issue. I'd learn later that patients are often reluctant to take medications for their thoughts and feelings. Psychiatrists are accustomed to this "refusal to take prescribed treatment." They approached the issue of taking medications slowly with patients, except in urgent cases such as psychoses, suicide attempts, or other illnesses in which the patient cannot function.

"Tell me about the attack."

I paused. I didn't want to remember it, afraid I'd feel it by describing it. Jack raised his eyebrows. I guessed that was a signal that I shouldn't hold back.

"I was trying to go to sleep. Then, my legs started feeling tingly and a numb feeling spread up my whole body. My heart was racing, and I felt like I couldn't breathe. I thought I was going to die." My voice broke.

"Was your husband with you?"

"Yes, he was asleep."

"Did you try to wake him up?"

"No," I said, surprised that he'd ask this. "Martin hates to be woken up from sleep."

"Don't you think he'd want to help you if you were having a crisis?"

I shrugged my shoulders.

"Tell me about your marriage."

I played with my wedding band. Jack's question confused me. I thought for a while, then decided to focus on numbers.

"We've been married almost ten years."

"Do you love him?"

"Yes, I do."

"Do you tell him that?"

"Yes. Well, I used to. But he doesn't respond when I say it. So I stopped saying it." Jack had to lean forward again to hear me.

"Does he love you?"

I looked beyond the doctor, annoyed that the once-white lace curtains largely obscured the view of the bare tree limbs outside.

"No."

Jack raised an eyebrow. "How do you know?"

"He won't tell me he loves me."

"Why?"

"He says he shouldn't have to tell me. He gets irritated when I ask him if he loves me."

"Why doesn't he like telling you he loves you?"

"He says he shouldn't have to. He says I'm too needy, that I should know how he feels."

"That's odd. I tell my wife every day that I love her."

Tears welled in my eyes. I couldn't stop them from dripping down my face. I didn't try to wipe them away. We sat there for a while, me crying, him watching, me hoping he didn't see the obvious tears.

"Tell me what you're feeling right now." It was a gentle command.

"I wish I was loveable, that someone could love me and tell me so." There was no hiding the tears now. Jack reached over to move the box of Kleenex closer to me. I grabbed a couple, soaked them immediately. I felt very embarrassed, wished I could jump up and run out of there. But wanting to be a good patient, I stayed.

"Why don't you think you're loveable?"

I shrugged. Jesus, why couldn't he let go of this? Couldn't he see how uncomfortable he was making me?

"Do your daughters love you?"

"Of course."

"So, you *are* loveable."

"Well, they're kids."

"Oh, so they don't know any better?"

I nodded.

"Do you love your mother?"

"No."

"So, it's not a given. Not every child loves her mother. Some mothers are loveable. Some are not."

I looked at him, surprised at this. I'd never thought of my girls loving me because of *me*. I thought they loved me because they had no choice—I was the only mother they had. And, I thought good people love their mothers, and my girls were wonderful children. I thought that I didn't love my mother because I was an evil person, not because she was unlovable. I didn't say any of this to Jack. I didn't want him to know how evil I was. It was bad enough that I'd just admitted to him that I didn't love my mother.

"Tell me about your mom."

"She hit me a lot."

"Tell me about it."

"The earliest one I remember happened when I was about three years old. I was home, so it must have been a weekend. I was feverish and crying. She slapped me when I didn't stop crying soon enough for her. The last one happened when I was eighteen years old. She hit me in the face with a pound of raw hamburger. She probably didn't hit me every day, but I worried every day because I couldn't tell what would precipitate a slap. I tried to be good, so she wouldn't hit me, but it never worked."

"That's so terrible. You didn't deserve that." Jack looked sad.

I shrugged. How did he know what I did or did not deserve? If I was evil, maybe I deserved to be beaten. My mother had told me she hit me for my own good. "Spare the rod, spoil the child" kind of thing.

Jack explained that mothers have lifelong effects on their children. I immediately worried that I was passing those effects on to my daughters. If my childhood permanently flawed me, how could I possibly be a good mother?

"Did you have any brothers or sisters?"

"No, there was just me."

"Were you afraid of your mother?"

Here came the tears again. Unable to speak, I nodded. Jack waited. Then he said, "Tell me about it."

"Once I turned seven, I came home alone after school. I was to come straight home, do my homework, and do my chores. I arrived home at 2:30. My mother called at 2:45 to make sure I was home and to remind me about the homework and chores. After the call ended, I'd raid the fridge and cupboard, bring my food into the living room, and settle down in front of the television. I'd watch the *Loretta Young Show* or *Adventures in Paradise*. Both were grown-up shows—there were no kids' shows on in the afternoon. If I had homework, I'd do it in front of the television. At 5:00, I'd turn off the television and remember the chores. I had fifteen minutes to peel six potatoes and put them on the stove to boil, defrost and cook hamburger, and sweep the kitchen floor. I learned how to speed things up, like cutting the potatoes small, and cooking the frozen hamburger on high heat. Sometimes, I'd forget to do one of the chores. My mother would start yelling when she got home, and then she'd slap my face, back and forth, back and forth."

Jack looked sad as I told this story.

"Last session, you said you lived with your mother and aunt. Tell me more about your aunt."

"Her name is Margie."

"She's your mother's sister?"

"Yes."

"Tell me about her."

"She's younger than my mother. She never married." I smiled. "She was fun when we lived together. She liked to joke around. She played games with me."

"So, she loved you."

"Yes. She called me her Anna Banana. She took care of me when I hurt myself or when I was sick."

Jack smiled.

"Once you were in first grade, you always lived with your mother and Margie?"

"Yes, until I was fifteen. Margie moved out then."

"That must have been hard. Why did she leave?"

There were the tears again. "She and my mother fought because my mother had started dating. Margie thought that she was sinning. Catholics are not allowed to divorce, so dating is a sin."

"You've had a hard life."

This shocked me. I thought my mother had the hard life, with losing her own mother to cancer when she was seventeen years old, marriage to an alcoholic who cheated on her, and then the responsibility of raising a child as a single mother in an era when few women were without husbands. She worked as an executive secretary for the regional office of a major oil company. As a woman, she had no hope of advancement in the company. She had to address the men as "Mister," while they called her "Mary." As she put it, she was stuck with an ungrateful brat of a daughter, which made her lot that much harder. And here I was, married ten years to someone who didn't drink to excess, didn't cheat, and was a wonderful father. I had two beautiful and delightful daughters. We had a split-level three-bedroom house in Westchester County on an acre of land. I had a PhD and was now working on an MD degree. How could he say I had a hard life? I wanted to ask him.

"You were abused as a child," he continued. "It was not your fault."

More tears. I'd cried more in the past half hour than in the last several years. What is this guy I wondered—some sort of sadist? Does he enjoy making women cry? I looked at the door. Maybe I should make a run for it.

"Were there any other family members in your life?"

"We were close to my granduncle. He lived about an hour south of Boston, near Cape Cod. We visited him a lot because he never married and didn't have children."

"What was his name?"

"Jake."

"Tell me about Jake."

"He was a sweet little old man. He loved to spoil me. He always gave me some of the pastries that neighbors brought him from the town bakery. And every time he saw me, usually once a week, he'd give me a dollar. That was a lot of money for him."

"Sounds like he loved you, too."

"Maybe. He never said it. He wasn't the hugging kind."

"We need to stop for today," he said gently.

I drove home slowly, confused at his continued questioning about my childhood. I didn't see how that related to my current problems. I tried to distance myself from the young Anne. She didn't exist anymore. As I drove, however, I thought about the parallels between her and my current self. Young Anne felt like she was in constant danger of being sent away by her mother and aunt. Adult Anne felt like she was in constant danger of her husband leaving her. Young Anne had to take care of her mother's moods and feelings. Adult Anne was responsible for her daughters' well-being and for keeping her husband happy. Young Anne did well scholastically but couldn't make or keep friends very well. Adult Anne struggled to keep up in her medical studies and felt like the odd person out in her class. Maybe the psychiatrist was right to look into my past.

I recalled that when I was about eight years old, my mother told me about my early childhood. She and my father split up when she was pregnant with me, and he gave up his parental rights. After I was born, she had the option of taking welfare or working. She chose to work, she said, because she didn't want to be a "welfare mother." She considered women on welfare to be cheap and low-class. When I was two months old, she returned to her secretarial job. She put me with a sitter during the day, but she said I woke her at night.

"You were disrupting my sleep," my mother said. I felt badly for her.

"So, I had to send you away," she continued. "I had no choice. You know, I thought about putting you up for adoption, but I decided to keep you. You were a beautiful baby—blonde and blue-eyed—you would have been adopted easily."

I guessed I was supposed to thank her for this. But inside, I wished she had decided differently. I knew an adopted girl; her parents doted on her.

Sometime later, she admitted that she'd kept me because she realized it would be her only chance at motherhood. As a Catholic, she was forbidden to remarry. She'd never again be able to have a child, unless she did the unthinkable and return to my father.

"I wanted to make sure I had someone to take care of me when I got old," she said.

The following day—Friday—was my mother-in-law's day to babysit. The girls enjoyed seeing her, and she loved the opportunity to see her son. Oh, I know she loved her grandchildren, but she adored her son. This became clear to me back when Martin and I were dating and visited his parents' house together. If Martin's mom and I were alone together, she tried hard to be pleasant with me. She'd ask me about my family and school and seemed interested. But if Martin entered the room, she'd start talking to him at once and ignore me. If I was in the middle of saying something, she didn't seem to notice, as if I ceased to exist at that moment.

When I told Martin that his mom didn't really like me, he said I was silly, that of course she liked me. He wouldn't discuss it. I had little hard evidence. She was always polite and kind to me. After we married, she included my name on the list of addresses in her weekly typed letters to her sons and daughters-in-law. She sent me birthday cards and gave me a Christmas present each year.

Corroboration of my feelings came from an offhand comment by his late father, when he once said, "No one loves the daughters-in-law. Parents love their sons. They love their daughters. They love their sons-in-law. But no one loves their daughters-in-law." I knew then that he was talking about his wife's feelings because I think he felt some affection for me. Maybe it was because he once patted me on my rear end. I interpreted that as affection, but maybe it was something else entirely. Perhaps he also did not love this daughter-in-law.

I could think of several reasons why my mother-in-law might not have liked me. I married her baby and took him away from her—to a new life, a new family, to Seattle (even though Martin's job offer at the University of Washington Department of Computer Science was the major factor driving us to choose Seattle). I came from a very different background than hers. My parents were divorced, and I'd grown up without a father. She and Martin's dad, married for forty years before his death, had admitted to me that they worried that I wouldn't be a stable life partner for their son. My family was working-class, not intellectual, not cultured. My in-laws considered themselves the opposite.

I wore a bikini in the summer and pants year-round. My mother-in-law dressed formally—always in a skirt, nylons, and a blouse, even when playing with her grandchildren. I drank beer out of a can. She neither drank alcohol nor served it in her home. I had nursed my daughters. She shuddered at the sight. I kept my maiden name—I think she took this as a personal insult that I rejected the family name.

She and I did share one thing in common. We were both worriers. She sat on the edge of her seat, body tense, as if readying herself to spring into action if needed. A nervous driver, she'd tentatively negotiate the New York and New Jersey thruways, swerving out of the path of merging cars and thereby risking collisions with those overtaking her. When Martin was in high school, she greeted him at the front door, no matter how late he came home. If he arrived later than his curfew, which he frequently did, she'd tell him she'd imagined him lying dead somewhere in a ditch. I could empathize with her anxieties. I was a wheel-gripping driver. And I imagined Martin lying dead if he arrived home more than ten minutes late.

She deserved her nervousness, I thought. She'd narrowly escaped the Holocaust and had fled from Vienna first to England at age eighteen to work as a domestic and then to New York before World War II. Her parents hadn't fared as well. Fleeing eastward from Austria, they'd been captured by Japanese and interned in a prisoner-of-war camp in the Philippines for the duration of the war. She and her parents were finally reunited following seven years of separation. Compared to her, I thought, I had no excuse for my worries.

I'd hoped to gain some points for bringing her baby closer to her when we came to New York for medical school. However, we'd made the mistake of stating that we planned to leave after I finished school in four years to return to Seattle. She hated me already for that.

I should have been grateful for the positive things my mother-in-law did for our family. She was a very generous woman. She loaned us $100,000 for my medical school tuition (we eventually paid it all back, with 5 percent interest). She also gifted each of our daughters a yearly sum of money, which we used for their educational expenses. There was no overt drama from this lady. She had only kind words for our family of four. She was polite and a skilled conversationalist. I was shy, abrupt, too ill at ease myself to realize how to help another person feel comfortable.

We had asked Martin's mother to babysit on Friday afternoons. I hadn't known any of my grandparents and thought it would be a good thing for the girls to spend time with their grandmother. She picked Cassie up at preschool, met Rachel at her bus, and passed the afternoon with the girls overseeing their play. When Martin arrived home, his mother hovered wherever he was, usually the kitchen. The girls loved their time with her and didn't seem bothered that her attention strayed to their dad when he was around. She stayed for dinner and drove home when Martin got too involved with the girls' bedtime to be able to focus on her.

As the days grew shorter and colder, her commute back to New Jersey was partly in the pitch black and often on icy roads. I worried about her maneuvering in those conditions. I suggested to her that she stay Friday nights at our house, so she wouldn't have to drive to New Jersey in the dark. She could travel home on Saturdays in the light. She was delighted. What I didn't foresee, however, was that she'd interpret that as an invitation to spend the entire Saturday with us, plus Saturday evening dinner. Her drive home, therefore, was still in the icy dark, but a full day later. As a result, I lost a weekend day with my family because Martin's mother needed her son to pay attention to her. So, Martin would spend time with her, I would be more responsible for the kids, and he would pretty much ignore me.

I should have been more empathic. My mother-in-law had been a widow for three years. Though she had many close relatives and friends, she returned home to an empty apartment. But I was jealously protective of the weekend with my husband. I wanted him and the girls to myself in the moments when I wasn't studying.

As a grandmother now, who babysits often for the grandchildren, I understand the feeling of wanting to talk with my daughters when they arrive home. But, knowing that my daughters' children need their moms more than I do, I try to bow out and leave soon. Now I can understand my mother-in-law's reluctance to leave her son each week; however, I still feel some guilt at my frustration with her at the time.

With the two girls, his mother, and his wife clamoring for his attention, Martin had a lot of female demands on him. I should have felt more sympathy for him. But at the time, I thought mostly of my own stresses.

On that Saturday night, Martin's mother stayed while we put the girls to bed. She chatted with Martin while I cleaned up the supper dishes. My annoyance existed on several levels. The dishes wouldn't get done on their own, and there were a lot of them. Then, I would need quiet to study and would have to retreat to our bedroom to concentrate. I worried that her voice would carry the twenty feet down the hall and through the thin wood door. Most of all, I wanted to talk with my husband. We'd been distracted with the girls all day, and then his mother demanded all his attention. As a result, he and I hadn't talked since Thursday evening. I wanted to connect with him, feel his affection for me even if he wouldn't say it.

While I steamed in the kitchen, her voice came closer.

"Good night, Anne," she said.

I barely looked up as I said goodbye. I didn't have the decency to thank her for sitting. If my rudeness upset her, she didn't let on. Martin helped her with her coat and walked her out to her car. A few minutes later he appeared and put his arms around me from behind. I stiffened.

"Why does she have to stay all day Saturday every week?" I asked.

"She's lonely," Martin said. "She loves seeing us."

"Well, I love seeing us, too, but it's impossible when she's here."

"What do you mean?" He seemed confused.

"You only pay attention to her when she's here." I was acting like a petulant child, no excuses.

"That's not true. I was with the girls all day. I even took them out for two hours, so you could study."

"Yes, and I appreciate that. I just don't want your mother around every week all Friday night and all-day Saturday into Saturday night. Can't you tell her she needs to go home Saturday mornings?"

"I can't do that. It would hurt her."

At this point, I had no sympathy for his poor mother. Then I thought of another tactic.

"Can we at least go out the night she's here, just the two of us? We can have a date night next Friday, go out to a restaurant."

Martin brightened at this. He loved going out to dinner, and this was a quick reprieve from this difficult conversation. He was off the hook. Or so he thought.

Chapter 14

Martin made reservations at Peter Pratt's Inn in Croton Heights for Friday night. Set in a Revolutionary War-era mansion, the restaurant was several steps above our usual family haunts. It was exactly a week after Valentine's Day; we had celebrated it as a kids' holiday—cards and sweets for the girls, nothing for us. I had turned thirty-three a couple of days before, which we'd marked with pizza at Lucy's Restaurant. The owner, whose niece was Cassie's best friend, had put a candle for me in a cup of chocolate gelato. Now, I felt like I was getting a second birthday celebration.

I wanted to look special for this rare date with my husband. I donned a red satin dress I'd made several years before but not worn for ages, surprised and happy that I could still zip it up. I carefully applied makeup, eye shadow, mascara, and lipstick. Then I attacked my hair with the curling iron. I wished I could do the stylish big hair of the times, but my limp locks decided differently.

Martin was giving the girls a bath. Martin's mother stood in the bathroom doorway talking to him. The girls talked to him at the same time. He wasn't a multitasker—I wondered which of the three voices he was processing.

I walked out of the bedroom as the girls burst from the bathroom wrapped in towels.

"Ooh, Mommy, you look so pretty," Rachel said.

"Yeah, Mommy's all fancy!" Cassie chimed in.

Martin's mother looked me up and down and smiled. I wondered if my dress and makeup were too flashy for her. We got the girls ready for bed, settled them down, and told them Grandma would read them a story, but they had to be quiet after she put the light out. They promised. I doubted it would work but was so excited about our night out that I didn't worry. If the girls stayed up too late, they'd just be a little cranky in the morning. I could handle cranky. We left the girls with Grandma and went into our bedroom for our final preparations.

Martin's gaze lingered on my face after he changed into a nice shirt and tie.

"What's that gunk on your face?" His face crunched into the expression he used when one of the toilets backed up.

"It's makeup, why?"

"It looks awful."

I turned and left the bedroom, crushed by his words. I felt like crying but didn't want to cause the awful-looking makeup to run down my face. Instead, I just walked into the girls' room to give them hugs and kisses goodnight. I slowly extricated myself from Cassie's clinging embrace, reassuring her that Grandma would take good care of her, and that we'd be home soon.

My stomach twisted in knots on the drive to the restaurant. The kind of knots that I knew would prevent me from eating. I wanted so badly for Martin to find me attractive and to tell me so. In my everyday life, I felt like a frumpy housewife. Tonight, I wanted to look special. I wanted to feel special.

I remained quiet on the drive, not wanting to share my feelings with

Martin. He'd get defensive, I knew, and would focus on how ugly makeup looks. It never occurred to me to explore why he so detested something that was associated with femininity in our culture. When he was a boy, all women wore makeup. His mother, teachers, and other women in his life must have at least worn powder and red lipstick. He abhorred perfume as well and felt faint when he walked through the fragrance section of a department store. But since he said something looked awful, I figured he must be right, that there was something wrong with me for wanting to apply cosmetics.

Once there, the charm of the restaurant's historic setting was lost on me. The privileged feeling of eating with wealthy people gave me no pleasure. The time alone with my husband lost its luster.

I ordered the mildest-appearing food on the menu, knowing I wouldn't want to eat it. Each course presented a new ordeal. Will a slice of bread calm my innards? Should I taste the appetizer or will it make things worse? Do I try the entrée or will it seem like cardboard to me, regardless of how many accolades the chef has received for his work? The wine, which usually calmed my nerves, tasted like vinegar so I left most of my glass untouched. I pushed food around my plate, the stomach pain too intense to put anything in my mouth other than a couple sips of water. When asked if I wanted dessert, the response was easy.

Martin noticed that I wasn't eating. "Is something wrong?" he asked.

"My stomach hurts," I replied.

"Oh, that's too bad." This was not the first time a stomachache had prevented me from enjoying a meal. It usually happened when one of the girls was upset, when Martin and I had had a fight, when I was worried about something, when my mother or aunt visited, or even when faced with a rude waiter. Since I'd started medical school, I often couldn't eat. (Unfortunately, I didn't lose weight. I downed too many sweets when my stomach recovered.) Still, a night out alone with Martin was usually a low-stress event, and my appetite responded with gusto. But not tonight.

I'd looked forward to this elegant, expensive dinner, and I hated every minute. I'd thought I was making myself pretty for my husband, but he let me know how ugly I was. Martin expressed sympathy for my stomach pain but didn't realize my discomfort was in reaction to his hurtful words. He didn't know because I didn't tell him.

At thirty-three years of age, I felt like an old woman. Surrounded by slim, fashionable, attractive female medical students, I felt like a middle-aged suburban matron. I weighed about 135 pounds at the time. At five feet, four inches tall, I was not a fat woman. But I felt fat, like the ugly, obese young girl I had been growing up. And outweighing many of my classmates by ten to twenty pounds made me feel even uglier. The fact that my husband never complimented me on my looks, but remarked on things he didn't like, made it much, much worse. How could I be attractive if even my husband found me repulsive?

Thankful to finally get home, I curled up in bed with a heating pad to rest my aching belly. The heating pad unfortunately didn't prevent panic attacks from occurring that night and the following night. The attacks made me feel like I'd been on super wash followed by maximum spin for hours. I was exhausted.

In the 1980s, anxiety was treated with tranquilizers, particularly the newer class of drugs called benzodiazepines. The most common at the time was Valium, which stayed in your system long enough to interfere with important things like mothering and studying. Jack offered me lorazepam, a shorter-acting benzodiazepine, meaning its effects can come on sooner and wear off sooner. He said it could short-cut my panic attacks and help me sleep. Skeptical of any drug that could affect my mind, I wasn't eager to take it. In college, I'd once paid a dollar to another girl in my dorm for a "downer." I didn't know where she got it, nor what the pill was. I swallowed the bright pink capsule with a mouthful of Ripple wine. The drug crept up on me slowly and kept me floating around the halls for a few hours. I couldn't afford to float now as a mom who needed to be there for her children and able to drive them safely without plowing into one of the charming stone walls that lined every country road near our house.

I was curious about this medication, however. The medical school curriculum didn't cover pharmacology until the second year, so I looked up lorazepam in a pharmacology textbook in New York Medical's library. I discovered that while it could calm panic attacks, it could cause excess sleepiness, dizziness, muscle weakness, and a host of other side effects that were not conducive to good mothering. A panic attack could also recur after the drug wore off. I never filled my lorazepam prescription, but I emerged with information about this class of drugs. I'd just experienced the heightened learning that medical students enjoy when faced with a real patient and a real treatment plan. Only in this case, I was the patient.

My reluctance to take this medication was not mirrored by others, I'd discover. The parents of one of my daughters' friends asked me if I could prescribe some lorazepam for them. "We like to take just a small dose. Just to take the edge off." I was shocked by this request. It was the first time anyone had asked me to prescribe something for them. So, I felt a little bit like a real doctor. However, their brazen request upset me. I wasn't their doctor and couldn't ethically prescribe something for a person I didn't take care of. Luckily, as a first-year medical student I had no ability to write prescriptions. That would not come until I'd finished medical school and at least one year of residency training, completed a series of medical knowledge exams, and been vetted by a state medical board as being a safe practitioner. I politely told them that I was not licensed to prescribe. I wondered if their friendliness toward me had been less about parents bonding than about the possibility of me being their drug supplier.

I know now that this class of drugs—benzodiazepines—can be very difficult to stop using. At the time, the pills probably would have helped me, perhaps allowing me to get some sleep. But they seemed too risky. While I rejected Jack's chemical medicines, I would accept his medicine of psychotherapy. It was the only choice I had.

Driving to Jack's on Monday afternoon, I thought about my need to feel pretty. It was an old feeling. Growing up in working-class Boston in the '60s, the main attribute of a Catholic girl was her looks. It defined her. If she was attractive, she could expect to marry a man with a good income, perhaps a plumber or an electrician. If she was plain, but had a nice personality, maybe she could land a streetcar conductor. If she was plain and shy, like me, she'd have no chance for marriage and had better make plans to support herself.

Girls in my school had been ranked according to their looks. A fat girl in my early teens, I ranked low. After I stopped eating in my mid-teen years and became thin, my ranking shot up enough to land me a boyfriend. Even when I became clinically underweight, however, I saw a fat, plain girl in the mirror. She stayed with me through college, marriage, pregnancies, motherhood, graduate school, and now into medical school. I desperately wanted to be pretty but saw only ugly in myself.

These feelings were diametrically opposed to the feminist I strove to be. I wanted women and girls to be appreciated for all their qualities, not just their looks. I thought that women deserved equal treatment to men in life, relationships, and employment. I had suffered from being treated as a lower class of human. In the Catholic church of my youth, women and girls were not allowed in the altar area. That holiest of areas was reserved for priests, deacons, and altar boys. It was as if we females were unclean. Few careers were open to women in those days. If I wanted to have a profession that required a college education, I would have to choose among being a schoolteacher, nurse, or librarian. When the Equal Rights Amendment failed, I felt doomed forever to be a second-class citizen.

I thought girls and boys should be treated alike. When Martin and I toured the Toronto hospital where our first daughter would be born, I was shocked to see that the boy babies were wrapped in blue blankets and girl babies were wrapped in pink. Even day-old infant girls were facing discrimination, by being visibly separated from boy babies. Then, after our daughter's birth, the nurses took her to the nursery where visitors could view the new arrival. Excitedly, I approached the nursery window to show off our new baby to some coworkers. I was horrified to see that she'd been mistakenly swaddled in blue. My thinking about girls and boys changed at that moment. I realized that I was proud of my little girl. I wanted to showcase her femininity, starting with a little pink blanket. I knocked on the window and asked the nurses to change her cover to pink.

I told Jack about the makeup debacle and my dinner experience.

"I couldn't eat," I said.

"Does this happen often, that you can't eat?"

"I can't eat if the girls are upset. Martin is often stern with them if they're not eating what we've prepared. As soon as he does this, I feel like my stomach shuts down. Then, if they start crying, I can't eat anything more at all. I just want to comfort them. They know this, and will get up from their seat to come over to me. That earns them another rebuke from Martin."

"Is he often hard on the girls?"

"He's strict. He never hits them, never yells at them. But he has firm thoughts about how children should behave."

"What do you love about your husband?"

I thought for a split second. "He's a wonderful dad, very responsible. He's witty and makes me laugh. He's stayed with me."

"Why wouldn't he want to stay with you?"

I shrugged. "I wouldn't think any guy would want to stay with me. I'm kind of boring. I'm not beautiful." I stopped there. There were so many reasons, too many to list.

"Could it be that he stays because he does love you?"

"No. He's just very dedicated to family. I'm family, the girls are family. Family comes first."

"So, you could be anyone, and he'd stay with you because you're family?"

"Yes."

We were both quiet for a minute.

"Could it be that you assume Martin will leave you because your father abandoned you completely, and your mother abandoned you when you were very little? Maybe you think Martin doesn't love you because your father was never there to love you?"

I looked away. If Martin loved me, why did he go to such extremes to avoid telling me he loved me? The thought that my parents' abandoning me could influence my insecurities about my husband surprised me. What other parts of my "reality" might be fake?

Jack disturbed my reverie. "Why don't you bring Martin with you next time you come? I have time at 11:00 this Saturday."

"I can ask." I doubted Martin would be willing to come. He'd never shown any interest in psychotherapy. I worried that this request would put stress on him, on our marriage. I worried it would send him running. And, with his mother staying over on Saturdays, there'd be the issue of his not being there for her.

That night, after the girls were in bed, I told Martin that Jack had said I should bring him to my next session.

"Sure," said Martin, to my surprise.

"We'll have to ask your mother to babysit," I said.

"Sure, I'll do that."

"Don't tell her we're seeing a psychiatrist. I'd like to keep that to ourselves." Martin's mother liked to share with her extended family. Within a couple of days, her sister, aunt, sister-in-law, nieces, and other son and daughter-in-law would know that I was mentally unstable and that my poor husband had to see the shrink to support me.

"Okay, I'll just say we have an appointment."

"She'll ask exactly what kind of appointment," I said. "Better to say we're visiting a friend."

"Okay."

Chapter 15

FEBRUARY 1986

The lives of my classmates looked so easy. After school, they'd saunter the 200 feet to their dormitory. There, they'd study for three hours before wandering down to the cafeteria for supper. Following this, maybe after a game of table tennis with their buddies, they'd be back at the books for another few hours.

My afternoons looked like this: After class, I'd drive to Yorktown Heights, stop at the A&P supermarket for milk, cheese, bread, and the few veggies the girls would eat. I'd pick up Cassie at her preschool and meet Rachel at her bus. I'd take them to their lessons—ballet or gymnastics or piano. I'd bring the girls home and start a laundry. I'd do some housecleaning depending on what looked the worst. The forest green rug in the living room tended to show lint, so I'd attack that with a vacuum. The bathrooms were often disaster areas, so I'd clean those at least once a week. I rarely got to the dusting. While doing these chores, I'd stage-manage the girls with their play and bickering. I'd worry about medical school and how I was falling far behind in my studies. I'd start supper, counting the minutes until Martin would arrive to take over the girls or the supper. Even with him home, I knew I wouldn't be able to study until at least 8:00 pm.

When I complained to Martin about all the housework, he said just don't do it. When I said the house would be disgusting, he said I was neurotic, that the bathrooms didn't need to be cleaned every week. That word—neurotic—was a conversation stopper for me. I didn't really know the meaning of the word, just that it had something to do with being mentally unhinged. The problem was me, not the amount of housework and the fact that I just didn't have time to do it all. The problem was that I thought about the house's cleanliness at all.

But think about it I did. I'd grown up in a house with two women. My mother and aunt couldn't have fixed a toilet to save their lives. But they knew how to clean. They worked full days during the week and were too tired at night to do chores. As a result, Saturdays were housework days: vacuuming, mopping, dusting, scouring the kitchen, cleaning the bathroom, scrubbing floors, and changing and washing sheets and towels. Anything less than this was slovenly. Being a child gave me no pass on the cleaning chores. I was expected to pitch in and help with every one of these tasks. We were poor, but we didn't have to be dirty.

I also had professional experience cleaning. At age fifteen, I'd worked as a maid at the Howard Johnson motel on Route 3 in Kingston, Massachusetts. I'd lived with my aunt that summer, and each day walked a half hour to and from the motel. We had systems and protocols for cleaning. We worked in pairs. One girl would strip the bed while the other would start in the bathroom. No one wanted bathroom duty, so we alternated. Some rooms were easy to clean. Our boss said those were the salesmen who stopped late, rose early, and used the room only to sleep. The party rooms were filthy. It amazed me how a room could be trashed in one night, with liquor spilled, cigarettes burned, and junk food scattered. Every surface would be covered in debris.

In college, I nannied for a wealthy family in Newton, a rich town west of Boston. My job included cleaning up after preteen boys who dropped towels and clothes on the floor as they finished with them; they knew a servant would take care of the discarded items. I was that servant.

Martin, on the other hand, was not expected to do any housework. That was women's work, and his family had his mother, his grandmother, and their weekly housecleaner to do this work. So Martin didn't notice dust, crumbs, or grime. He never had to—that was someone else's job. He decided my noticing these things was a sign of neurosis. What if, instead, his not noticing dirt was a manifestation of the privileged childhood he'd had as a male in a well-to-do family? My problem was that I didn't realize that my wish to keep a clean house was perfectly normal, not a sign of insanity. I was so willing to accept that I was an aberration.

He and I had different views of how a home should look. He valued neatness, I valued cleanliness. It was difficult for him to have the order he craved without involving others in the family, so I gradually changed from a rather messy person to a less messy one. There was no feng shui in vogue back then. We didn't have books and streaming television shows telling us how tidiness is life-changing. Now, as a less messy person, order calms me. When Martin insisted on order in our early days of marriage, it infuriated me.

When our older daughter was just old enough to grab toys from her toy box and scatter them as she crawled around, the living room looked like a multicolored plastic bomb had detonated. When Martin arrived home from work, he'd get down on the floor to put all the toys away before he'd pay attention to his daughter. This bothered me on many levels. First, I wanted his daughter to have a dad who cherished her without condition, including the condition that she be neat. I wanted a husband to take this kid who velcroed herself to my hip each afternoon. I wanted some relief so I could finish making the now-soggy pasta and burnt-on spaghetti sauce; we could eat by six o'clock, our daughter could have her bath at 6:30, I could nurse her at seven, put her down to sleep at 7:30, and read on the couch until I fell asleep there at 8:30. To counter his neatness-before-fatherhood habit, I began tidying the mess before he came home. At first Rachel thought it was a fun game and would crawl to the toy box to dislodge anything I'd flung in there. I changed my strategy to do the clean-up with her firmly in my left arm while I organized with my right. I realize now that I enabled his obsession, instead of telling him that it would be really nice if he'd play with his daughter and ignore the chaotic living room floor.

Alternatively, perhaps part of me craved the order he brought to our lives. Maybe I straightened up our house in an attempt to straighten up my mind.

My patience about the housecleaning issue finally wore out as the next set of medical school exams approached.

"We need to hire a cleaner," I announced one day as soon as Martin came through the front door.

He stopped and stared. It wasn't my usual greeting.

"It's not necessary," he said. "We don't need a cleaner."

"I can't handle all this anymore. I have to study, or I'll flunk out of school. I have no time at all in the afternoons to study. Then at night I'm so tired I'm falling asleep on my books."

"You're just neurotic. The house looks fine."

"It looks fine because I'm cleaning it!" By now my voice was raised, unusual for me. Martin stood stock still.

"Your mother always had a maid," I continued. "Why was it okay for her to have a maid, even though she only worked half-time? I'm studying full-time, but I'm expected to do all the housework." I conveniently omitted the cooking, dishwashing, and laundry from the housework equation. Martin was wonderful about sharing these fifty-fifty with me, but my issue now was the time I spent on cleaning.

"Just stop cleaning. No one is expecting it."

"I need a cleaner." My voice was quiet by now. Ominous maybe.

"How much will it cost?"

"I don't know. I'll find out." This was a lie. I had no intention of doing the math, of figuring out whether we could afford it. I had a dream-like vision of making a fortune once I had my medical degree, so it didn't bother me to go into debt a little while I was in training. I didn't consider where these funds would come from, whether Martin's monthly salary could stretch to pay for mortgage plus food plus the girls' needs plus all the varied costs of running our lives. We had no savings at this point and lived paycheck-to-paycheck. Perhaps I was reaching into my Catholic past and expected a loaves-and-fishes sort of thing—that money would somehow expand to cover our needs. I saved my logical thinking for medicine and applied magical thinking to finances. At the time, I didn't appreciate that Martin's financial conservatism saved us from serious debt.

Martin didn't say anything else. I took this as a "yes," because I wanted a yes, not because Martin ever conceded by keeping quiet.

I asked the few women I knew in Yorktown Heights—our real estate agent, our lawyer, the neighbor whose daughter babysat for us, the mom of one of Cassie's friends—for leads. One of them led me to a woman whom I hired without any further discussion with Martin. She would save my life every other Wednesday, turning my dirty house into a sparkling home. And if she was still there when I arrived home, we'd have a cup of tea together and talk about our children and husbands.

I never felt completely comfortable with the relationship, however. As a former domestic worker, I felt like I should be the cleaner, not the boss. I had trouble telling her exactly how I wanted things done. Furthermore, I didn't know exactly what I wanted until something didn't look quite right. I also felt embarrassed about giving specific instructions—like who was I to tell someone else how to do their job? I did tell her to stop waxing the Italian tiles that ran the length of the house, but that was only after Cassie took a fast fall at the end of a twenty-foot skid and almost cracked her head open.

Still, this arrangement freed several hours per week for study time, and it significantly reduced my stress. I had someone to help me. I wasn't alone.

My discomfort with directing the housecleaner was not a surprise. I routinely cleaned up when we stayed in hotels, so the maids wouldn't think I was burdening them. I rarely complained in a restaurant and never sent food back. Martin would need to deal with repairmen because I couldn't be trusted to check their work and insist on job completion. I never accepted the grocery store baggers' offers to bring the groceries to my car. I was forever the peasant, never the princess.

Our scheduled Saturday morning appointment with Jack arrived. Martin's mother walked us to the front door. It felt as if she wanted this to be her home, and she the woman of the house. The girls tried to get her attention to read them a story. I wondered if she knew we were going for marriage counseling, and if she hoped it wouldn't work. I had a lot of thoughts going through my mind on the way to our appointment. What if Martin hates him, hates the process? What if he gets angry about anything Jack says? Jack had gently given me advice, and I assumed he'd do the same with Martin. Martin didn't do well with people telling him what to do. But maybe he would do okay with another man guiding him. In the past, I'd noticed that he seemed more comfortable taking suggestions from male friends or relatives.

I worried how Jack would treat Martin. I'd not painted the most flattering picture of my husband. I wasn't accustomed to talking about my spouse. I had few friends and didn't feel close enough to any of them to talk in depth about my personal life. The only exception was my sister-in-law, with whom I shared the experience of marriage to brothers who had many similarities. She and I loved our husbands, so our talk was more about how different these men were from the typical North American men. Instead of the American "god, country, family," the brothers' European Jewish parents raised their children to value intellect, ethics, and family. Their families had given up their Jewish religion in Europe in hopes of avoiding persecution. (It didn't work, and they were forced to flee or perish.) His parents felt little allegiance to their birth countries of Austria and Hungary, given the rampant anti-Semitism there. Instead, they had a strong moral compass. This was not based in religion. Rather, it was based on the idea that they should act according to the right thing to do. They were strictly honest. If a waiter forgot to add an item to a bill, they brought it to the waiter's attention. They were diplomatic and collegial. Most importantly, family came first, always. Martin's parents hosted weekly family gatherings at their house, rain or shine. All relatives were welcome to join the weekly events of coffee, Viennese cakes, games, and classical music. Years later, we'd learn that his parents provided financial support to a wide range of relatives, never saying "no" to a request to help with someone's tuition, rent, or a medical expense.

The session with Jack went surprisingly well, except that I didn't enjoy being the object of conversation. Jack asked Martin how he felt during my panic attacks. Martin said he felt helpless, which surprised me. I thought he had it all together while I was falling apart. Jack gave Martin pointers on how to help me with them. Mostly it involved holding me—Jack was big on hugging. Toward the end, we talked about money.

"She wastes money on clothes," Martin said.

Jack looked him straight in the eye. "You need to let her buy things for herself. It's really important for her."

Martin nodded. For the first time, I was happy to be in therapy. Someone was on my side.

Jack suggested that we come in once a week for couples' therapy. I was grateful to hear Martin agree to this. After all, I was the crazy one.

Over the years in my career as a physician and researcher, I have been through many situations in which my gender has held me back. Things like the male boss who slapped my knee at the end of a meeting. The skin on my knee hurt for an hour, but the hurt to my self-esteem stung for years because I knew that if I said anything about it, the repercussions would be harsh. And like the female boss who told me I should stay quiet on study conference calls. There was the time I learned another physician in my organization made many thousand dollars more per year than I; my boss refused to consider equity. I had to obtain an outside job offer, and go through a faculty promotion process, before I received my "equity" raise. If I acted in an assertive manner, I was labeled a problem. The same assertiveness in a man would be considered appropriate.

If a therapist today told Martin to "let" me spend money on myself, I'd be furious. The implication was that Martin oversaw finances, and I was the little girl being given an allowance. At the time, however, when I felt like I was in control of nothing in my life, it helped to have one man in my life tell another that he needed to allow me this.

Chapter 16

MARCH 1986

The process with Jack was going to be slow, I realized. I'd hoped for a quick diagnosis and cure. That wasn't going to happen. I still had panic attacks. While they didn't happen every day, I also couldn't predict what would set one off. I might be sitting quietly, studying, when I'd start to feel the heart racing, sweating, numb extremities, I'm-about-to-die sort of feeling. Or I'd be exhausted, lying in bed, knowing I had to get to sleep right then and there or else I'd have to function the next day on only six hours of sleep or five hours of sleep or four hours or no sleep. And then the panic would ensue. But other times I could be having the same dark thoughts and not have a panic attack. It was as if my body and mind had been invaded by an evil spirit who sat in wait until I was at rest, unaware. He'd then strike with full force. It kept me on edge all the time, not knowing when or where I'd panic. This is a basic tenet of psychological torture—keep the victim in suspense. You don't have to abuse the person constantly—just let her feel threatened at all times so she can never relax. I never relaxed.

Part of me wanted to go back in time, before medical school. We could return to Seattle and I could be "just a mom." Maybe I could get a part-time clerical job to bring in a few more dollars. I could quit therapy, stop trying to push myself to change my entire way of dealing with life stresses. But there was no guarantee that the panic attacks would stop. At some point, I'd face other life stresses, and my persistent anxiety could once again explode to panic mode.

There was no turning back. At the same time, I feared going forward.

One day Jack asked me if I had experienced anxious feelings earlier in my life.

"I guess I was a nervous kid," I replied.

"How so?"

"I panicked if I had to stand in front of the class to recite anything." My hands clenched at the memory.

"What did it feel like?"

"My heart pounded. My throat went dry. I could feel myself blushing deep red." As I spoke, I felt all of these symptoms as if I were back in third grade.

"Were there other times you felt like this?"

I jumped a little, half expecting Sister Sophia to have asked the question. "Oh, all the time. Anytime a Sister called on me. In the schoolyard. When my mother came home from work. In church, waiting to say my Confession."

"What made you uneasy about Confession?"

Okay, I thought, this guy clearly isn't Catholic.

"Confession is you going into a tall wooden box and talking to God. You confess all your sins, all the big and little things you are ashamed of. Things you wouldn't tell your best friend. And here you are face-to-face with God, who's separated from you by just a thin wall with a little screen."

"I'm Jewish," Jack said, "so I've only seen Confession in movies. Don't you tell your sins to the priest?"

"Exactly, and the priest is God on earth, God's messenger. We treated the priests like they were God, and they expected to be treated like they were God."

I pulled at a strand of hair for a minute, then continued.

"I was terrified of the priests. First, they were all men, and men scared the bejesus out of me. The priests also had the power to inflict punishment. A priest could decide my sins warranted a stiff penance. He could make me come to church every day after school and kneel at the altar for hours, reciting prayer after prayer. Everyone would know what a terrible sinner I was. To avoid this, you had to confess enough to satisfy the real God, but not so much that you'd be given a stiff sentence by the priest."

"Why were you so afraid of men?" Jack asked. He wrote something on a piece of paper inside an off-white file folder that he balanced on his crossed knee.

Really? Of all the material I just handed him—nuns, priests, God, the confessional, the schoolyard, my mother—he zeroed in on men? Okay, I thought, it must be important.

"I guess I didn't know anything about men. I'd lived with only women—my mother and aunt. Even my time in boarding homes was primarily with women. The first one was operated by a woman with questionable qualifications. A nurse owned the second home and she hired other nurses to help. Nuns ran the boarding school and the boarders were girls. My babysitters were female, and my teachers were all nuns."

I hesitated, then continued. "I learned early that men rule the world. They're the presidents and managers, the writers and doctors, the lawyers and the union bosses. They make laws and make arrests. They decide who lives and who dies. Most dangerous criminals are men. When I arrived home to an empty house as a kid, I worried that a bogeyman would be hiding under my bed. Not a bogeywoman."

I paused again. This was a long speech for me. Usually I thought things through in my head and blurted out the summary statement as if the other person could intuit my stream of thought.

"Many girls learn about men from their fathers. But you didn't really know yours, did you?"

"No, I met him first when I was a teenager."

"He was not in your life at all before that?"

"My mother told me that he would visit me sporadically when I was a baby or toddler, but the visits stopped when I was four years old. My mother said he would promise to visit, I'd wear my prettiest dress, and watch out the window long after he failed to show up."

"Tell me how you finally met him. Did he instigate that or did you?"

"I did. I sent him a Christmas card."

"That must have been hard for you."

"Yeah, my mother wasn't happy about it. I had to ask her for his address. Then, he didn't answer for weeks. I thought he had no interest in me at all."

"He finally responded?" Jack stroked his mustache.

"He called my mother and said he'd like to see me. So, my mother and I met him in a local bar."

"Wow, I'm surprised your mother would bring you to a bar and that the bar would let you in."

"It was 1969, before the drinking age went up. Maybe they thought I was eighteen."

"What was it like seeing him for the first time?"

"It was surreal. I'd seen pictures of him as a younger, handsome man. This guy was middle-aged, with horn-rimmed bifocals, and a little pot belly. It was strange to hear his voice. It was raspy, a smoker's voice. He barely looked at me, just talked with my mother about his job and people they both knew. He said what a great man Richard Nixon was."

Jack laughed. "Did you see him again after that?"

"Yes. He came to my high school graduation. Then, when I went to college in Boston, I'd often drop in to his house in Newton. I sang at his wedding. I asked him to pay for my wedding. He insisted on walking me down the aisle."

"Do you see him now?"

"Only about once a year when we go to Massachusetts to visit my mother and aunt. We take a half day to visit my father and his wife."

"So, your girls have met him?"

"Yeah, a couple of times. He's a lot of fun to be with—the girls really took to him."

"How does that make you feel?"

I took a deep breath. "Jealous. I wish he'd been there for me when I was a little girl."

"Did he visit you in Seattle? Or here in New York?"

"No, never."

"Does that disappoint you?"

"Yeah." I took another deep breath.

"What's your relationship like now?"

"Kind of weird. There's this man who gave me DNA but has no idea how to be a parent. It's like having half a dad. He coughed up only half of his twenty dollars a week child support the court required him to pay. Once, in college, I had a bike accident and struck my head on some streetcar tracks. I called my father to get me. He said he couldn't because he was at work. I said I had no one else—my mother lived more than an hour away. In the end, he picked me up and took me to the emergency room, but he kept repeating that he'd get in trouble with his boss. Then later, when I decided to buy a car instead of relying on a bike, he helped me find a used car. But he didn't offer any money to help with the costs. He was kind of a half-assed dad."

"Is there anything you like to do with him?"

"He's good for drinking. He and his wife are generous with their liquor. From him, I learned to drink Chivas Regal on the rocks."

"Does he drink a lot when you see him?"

"Always. For my eighteenth birthday, he and his wife took me to dinner at Marliave's, my favorite restaurant in Boston. He drank so much that his foot sat on the brake on the entire drive home. When we arrived at my dorm, he got out of the car. Before I knew what was happening, he kissed me, open mouthed, with tongue. I pulled away and ran off. I didn't thank him for the nice birthday dinner."

I felt dirty just telling Jack about this. I'd never told anyone about it before. I almost thought I'd imagined it.

"Did you ever say anything to him after that about the kiss?" Jack asked.

"No. I just never let my face get near him when there was a hello or goodbye hug."

"I don't think you had even half a dad. He failed you in so many ways. And it wasn't your fault."

That brought out my tears. Jack sure knew how to make a girl cry.

I knew very little about Jack. He said that therapy is all about the patient and that usually the therapist says nothing about their own life. He said he made a slight exception for me and told me some things about his family so that I could understand that it's okay to talk about mine. He'd been married for over two decades and loved his wife. He had three children. He'd graduated from New York Medical College. He told me about his distant mother and loving father. This helped me understand it's okay to think and talk about the ways your parents fail you and that you can succeed in marriage, parenthood, and career even if you were dealt abusive, uncaring, or problematic parents.

Yet, I didn't want to know much about Jack. Once I saw him in his car pulling into a shopping mall. My heart pounded; I wanted to hide. I told him about this at our next session. He said it was not surprising.

"Transference," he said. "It's not uncommon for patients to have feelings for their therapists. They transfer aspects of their parents onto their therapists. Since you've searched for a dad all your life, your mind transforms me into a father figure."

At my sessions, I'd often report on that week's medical school stresses. I'd insist that I couldn't manage it all, that my mom duties took up all my time leaving no time to study. Jack would insist that I could do it. He suggested that I join a study group with other students. I responded with the facts—I didn't have time to do this. It was getting to be an old refrain: I'd say I can't do this all; he'd say yes, you can. Sometimes, I'd leave therapy more stressed than when I went in because Jack urged me to spend more time away from the books.

While Jack understood the demands of medical school and he himself was a parent, he had not combined them at the same time. And he wasn't a mom. For children, a dad reading was busy, not to be disturbed. A mom with her head in a book, on the other hand, was just biding time until one of her children needed her attention. I didn't believe Jack's optimism about my abilities to fit the studying into the limited time available.

Looking back, I can understand his rationale. I felt like I was facing a behemoth on my own, with no one to guide me, no one to assist me. I was the reluctant hero on a journey with no map or signposts, and I was running out of fuel. Maybe a study group would have helped me feel less isolated. But at the time, I could only think of my lack of time and lack of brain power. I never did join a study group.

Often, when I told Jack about some recent episode of stress, he'd ask, "How does that make you feel?" This was one of his favorite questions, and the one I hated most of all. It was hard enough to talk about my current situations and relationships. But to then tell him how I felt—it was torture.

"Tell me more about your worry that Martin will leave you," Jack said at one session.

"I don't know. I just assume he'll find someone better and want to be with her. Or he'll get tired of my mess or my anxiety or my wanting things, and he'll want to get away from me."

"Has he ever left you?"

"No, not since we married."

"Has he ever threatened to leave?"

"No, never."

"Has he ever had an affair?"

"No, not that I know of."

"And he moved out here to New York to be with you, to make you happy."

"Yes." Tears again.

"So, your fears of him abandoning you are not based on your experiences with him."

"I guess not."

"Your mother abandoned you when she sent you to live in other homes and institutions. And your father abandoned you completely.'

I just looked at him. I'd realized my experiences were odd but didn't realize I had been abandoned.

"The trauma caused by your abandonment is still with you. You expect people you love to leave you because that's all you know. But you can change your way of thinking, and Martin and I can help you."

I certainly hadn't realized I'd been the victim of childhood trauma. I thought of children who'd been in orphanages as trauma victims. But when I mentioned that I'd thrown up every morning at the Catholic boarding school where I lived for my kindergarten year and lost a significant amount of weight while there, he said I'd experienced emotional and physical trauma.

"You could have died," he said.

At the time, I didn't know that anxiety disorders are the largest group of mental disorders and are a leading cause of disability. The Anxiety and Depression Association of America estimates that forty million American adults—almost one in five individuals—suffer from an anxiety disorder each year. US surveys find that 40 percent of women will develop an anxiety disorder in their lifetimes. The risk of developing a generalized anxiety disorder, my kind of anxiety, is almost one in twelve women. The lifetime risk of a panic disorder is one in fourteen women. I had a lot of company, but since most people with an anxiety disorder are never diagnosed by a doctor, it didn't feel like I had a tribe of similar people.

Anxiety disorders usually begin in childhood, adolescence, or early adulthood. Untreated, these disorders tend to be chronic, with periods of higher or lower levels of symptoms depending on life stressors. The disorders are more common in girls and women than in boys and men. Individuals who have experienced childhood physical or sexual abuse, parental separation, or emotional maltreatment are at higher risk. People whose family members suffer from anxiety or depression are more likely to develop an anxiety disorder. I had experienced most of these risk factors. It's no wonder I developed an anxiety condition.

Several gene variations have been identified that may place people at high risk for these disorders; if you inherit such a variation from a parent, you can inherit his or her anxiety. However, it's difficult to tease apart the effect of that gene from the effect of the parenting style and

CHAPTER 16

life circumstances you grew up with. In other words, if you have a gene variation that can increase risk but you have the perfect childhood family life, will that nurturing overcome the effect of the gene?

Life stressors in young adults can augment symptoms significantly. In the past year, I'd quit a job, moved from Seattle, settled in New York, started an overwhelmingly difficult educational program, all while trying to provide support to my husband and daughters who were also stressed from these changes. I guess these all could count as life stressors.

Scientists have discovered several parts of the brain that can drive the abnormal fear and anxiety responses in persons with anxiety disorders. These include areas of the amygdala, hippocampus, medial prefrontal cortex, hypothalamus, midbrain, and brainstem. So basically, my whole brain was over- or under-functioning. It's a wonder I retained anything I studied.

Much of the laboratory research on anxiety has been conducted in rats. While many things cause fear in rats, juggling medical school and motherhood is not one of them. Animal studies can only take us so far in understanding how humans respond to stress. Newer technology that allows doctors to scan patients' brains safely has helped to pinpoint areas of the brain that can be over- or under-stimulated in people with histories of traumas such as childhood abuse.

Mental health professionals diagnose anxiety disorders by their clinical presentation, using criteria laid out in the current version of the *Diagnostic and Statistical Manual* (*DSM*), sort of a psychiatric bible. While that helps with designing a treatment plan and getting insurance reimbursement, it doesn't cover the nuances of psychiatric care needed for an individual patient. That's where the art of psychiatric treatment comes in. I was like a block of clay with spikes all over that Jack was trying to mold back into some semblance of a well-adjusted mom and future doctor. He'd need significant artistic skills.

Most people with anxiety disorders never seek the care of a professional, but rather deal with their uncomfortable or terrifying symptoms on their own. Some self-treat with alcohol or illicit drugs. Others avoid stressors, and sadly miss out on some life joys. Others may find help through calming activities such as prayer, meditation, yoga, or exercise. For those patients who seek help, psychological therapy has been shown to help in as little as ten weeks. Medications can help some people, but there are side effects and costs to deal with. Often, professionals recommend a combination of both medications and psychotherapy. While many patients improve with therapy, symptoms can recur with future life stressors. Some anxiety patients unfortunately develop depression and others become addicted to alcohol or other drugs. As a result, anxiety disorders are usually chronic diseases that will need repeated management over a person's lifetime.

Just before the time when I suffered in New York, Seattle researchers studied the effect of medical school on students' mental health. They published results of their study in 1984. These scientists found that of 605 first-year medical students at the University of Washington, over a third reported symptoms of anxiety at the beginning of the school year that were well above those seen in patients with known mental illnesses. Many of their symptoms were linked to the stress of mastering knowledge, competition with other students, long hours of study/work, and feelings of anonymity, perceived threat, and lack of control over their own lives. Women had higher levels of distress than men. The researchers found that levels of anxiety increased over the first year of medical school, and those students who were more anxious early in the year had the greatest levels of anxiety at the end of the year. In a more recent summary of research on medical students' mental health, married students were found to have lower stress levels than unmarried students. There was no information on the effect of having children on levels of stress or anxiety, but there was a suggestion of increased risk for depression in mothers in medical school. A recent study found that medical students in New York were eight times more likely to have generalized anxiety disorder than the general population.

It's likely that many medical students were dealing with similar experiences to mine. Unfortunately, most medical schools at the time didn't recognize that large numbers of their students were in distress, nor did they develop programs to help students avoid the ravages of anxiety and other mental illnesses. Students like me were on their own.

My therapy sessions felt like Jack was peeling a boiled egg to uncover what was underneath. I'd developed defenses, he told me. My childhood was so fraught with dangers—I'd be abandoned again, sent away, beaten— that I'd built ways to protect myself. It would hurt less for people to leave me if I didn't allow myself to attach so closely to them. That I found someone willing to marry me and that I was able to commit to him, was surprising. (Jack never said this—I surmised it from all I was learning about myself.) My choice of a man who wouldn't tell me he loved me fit with my own emotional limitations. Perhaps I was attracted to a man who wasn't in touch with his feelings because I buried my own feelings. Maybe my toe-dipping into emotions could help my husband as well as me.

As Jack gently helped me unwrap my defensive layers, I resembled an egg where the white sticks to the shell, leaving a lumpy, ugly mass. I worried that my inner thoughts and feelings would stink if exposed.

In our clinical medicine class, we learned how to write notes on our patients, to document their problems, our diagnoses, our plans for their care, and how they were responding to treatment. One format was called the SOAP note, which stands for subjective (S) information, objective

(O) data, assessment (A), and plan (P). This documentation was originally developed by physicians, for physicians, as historically they were the only ones allowed to write in a patient's chart.

The subjective information section is a brief statement of the patient's purpose for coming to the doctor or hospital. The objective section includes information that the physician assesses during a physical examination. The physical examination findings and any laboratory or radiological test results would follow. The assessment area is where the physician speculates about a possible diagnosis and about how the patient is doing. The plan documents what the medical team will do for the patient. It includes medications prescribed, tests and procedures to be performed, and long-range plans.

If someone were to write a SOAP note on me at that time, they'd begin with my subjective complaint: "I keep having these attacks where my whole body goes numb and I can't think and I can't function and my heart feels like it's going to explode out of my body and I can't breathe." The objective part could read: "Patient is a thirty-two-year-old female who appears to be in acute psychological distress. Her affect is anxious, sitting on the edge of the chair, hands clenched. She speaks softly in a halting voice." The assessment would probably say, "Generalized Anxiety Disorder with Panic Attacks." The plan might be along the lines of psychotherapy with or without medication. The problem was that I didn't know how long the plan would take, what it would entail, or whether it would even work. Still, I saw no alternative other than seeing this strange but kind doctor twice weekly and hoping for the best.

Chapter 17

MARCH 1986

"Please, Mom, please!" Rachel implored. "Katie's mom lets her do it."

There it was—the best-friend's-mom defense. It was one of the most powerful rationales employed by daughters. The problem was that it worked very well on me. I was so unsure of myself, of my decision-making, that I could be easily swayed by the knowledge that another mom would allow something.

The "it" in this case was to take horseback riding lessons. This request took me by surprise. While the frequent stables I passed driving the roads of Westchester told me I was in horse country, I'd thought equestrian activities were limited to rich people. We weren't rich people. The best friend Katie, who went to the same public school as Rachel and lived in a split-level ranch house like ours, did not appear to be rich. So, what was she doing on a horse?

It turned out that taking riding lessons didn't mean you had to own a horse. You just had to cough up the costs for weekly lessons on a school horse. The students were required to wear helmets, but they could borrow them from the school. Riding boots would be needed later; to start, Rachel could wear sneakers.

I'd only been on a beast once. When I was nine years old, the YMCA took the summer day campers to a fair. I waited in line with two of my friends and twenty other kids for a ten-minute ride on one overworked pony. A big sign announced a 100-pound weight limit. I was pretty sure that of the pack of waiting kids, I was the only one over the weight limit. First, I panicked at the thought that the operator might have a scale at the front and my shameful weight would be broadcast. When I saw that there was no scale, I had to decide between being honest to save the health and welfare of the animal versus pretending I weighed less than the load limit. I chose the latter. For the entire ten-minute ride, pony tethered to a lead rope and plodding around a ring, I worried that I would cause irreparable damage to this poor little creature. Or, even worse, I worried that he'd drop beneath me of exhaustion. My secret of exceeding the weight limit would be exposed. I'd be shamed as fat, dishonest, and cruel to animals. Now in medical school, just as I'd over-burdened that pony, I was putting too much weight on myself.

In the intervening years, I'd never had exposure to horses, never even considered getting on an animal myself. And I certainly didn't think of my little girls going anywhere near a horse. Martin was fine with the request. "It's wholesome," he said. Hmm, how was a head split open, with blood and brain spilling out onto dung-stained wood shavings wholesome? (I pictured every ride ending this way.) I'd later learn that my worries were in line with the science: equestrian sports cause almost half of traumatic brain injuries in this country. Horseback riding is more dangerous than motorcycle riding.

The "best-friend's-mom-allows" argument and the "wholesome" reasoning won out over my better judgement. Rachel began lessons with her friend at a stable near Yorktown Heights. Because Cassie had to do whatever her older sister did, she began lessons also. The outside of the stable looked like the wooden façade of a Hollywood western town. Inside was a large ring covered in something that resembled synthetic sand and surrounded by bleachers behind a five-foot wooden wall. I was happy to see that the wall would separate me from the giant animals. The arena was filled with big horses and little girls. I wondered why this sport was populated primarily by girls in this country. I imagined the girls wanting to control a big beast since they couldn't control their parents. Rachel enjoyed riding for the next couple of years, while she remained friends with Katie. Our younger daughter Cassie, however, continued to ride for many years. Luckily, neither girl suffered any of the extreme injuries I imagined could happen in this sport.

As I worried about my girls on the backs of large animals they didn't yet know how to control, I rode my own beasts. Medicine was a monolithic institution with immense powers over its doctors-in-training. I had no idea how to handle it, could barely hold on as the ride galloped through anatomy, physiology, and the myriad things that can go wrong in the human body and the means to fix them.

I held myself together most days. The girls, especially, kept me focused on the present. I could think about ballet costumes and dolls and drawing without perseverating about my own schoolwork and likelihood of failing. Supper and evening activities were equally distracting. It's hard to panic when you're washing a little girl's beautiful mane of long red hair. After the girls were finally asleep, I could focus on my studies.

The troubles started as I lay in bed thinking about how I couldn't do all I was trying to do and how I'd fail and how ashamed I would be. Then, the panic attacks would creep in. One night, remembering what Jack had recommended, I woke Martin when I was in full panic mode. This was difficult because during an attack, my body felt frozen, as if I were stuck in a paralyzing dream. To move, I pretended I was moving someone else's body. It felt like manipulating a marionette.

"Huh," he mumbled.

"I'm scared," I said.

"Huh?"

"I'm having one of my attacks," I said. I may have shouted.

He sat up, blinked, and reached for his glasses. He looked at me. I sat, looking straight ahead, shivering. He put his arm around me and pulled me over to him. I leaned against him, still shaking. This wasn't helping at all, I realized.

"I need to talk to Jack," I said.

"Okay," Martin said.

I reached over to my purse and, with trembling hands, pulled out my address book. I could barely turn the pages.

"Can you call for me?" I asked.

"Sure." Martin reached for the phone on his bedside table and dialed the number. I heard him talking with the answering service.

"She said she'll give him the message."

"I can't wait that long." Shouting again.

"She said you could call the mental health emergency line."

"Okay, what was that number?"

"I don't know."

"Can you call her back?"

He got the number for me. This time I dialed for myself. I was standing up by now, freezing cold but too numb to think about getting myself a sweater or blanket.

"I'm having a panic attack," I told the person who answered. She passed me along to a counselor.

"Hi," he said. "I'm Steve. I'm the psychiatrist on duty. What's your name?"

"Anne."

"Hi Anne. What seems to be the trouble?"

"I'm having a panic attack, and I can't reach my psychiatrist."

"Okay, I'm sorry you're feeling badly. First, I want you to remember that the panic attack will pass."

Hearing his warm, kind voice made me feel a little better already.

"Can you tell me what you're feeling now?" he asked.

I described the symptoms.

"Okay, why don't we slow your breathing down a little. Take a slow breath in, hold it for a count of three, and then let it out for a count of eight."

We did this for a few minutes. My heart rate slowed, almost to normal. He asked if my doctor had given me any medications for my panic attacks. I said I couldn't take anything that would make me too drowsy. He suggested I talk with my doctor again about something to use at night. He said to see my doctor as soon as I could and to call the emergency number again if I needed help sooner. I thanked him and hung up.

I looked over to the bed. Martin was asleep, snoring. This enraged me. I wanted him to be awake and suffering along with me. At the same time, I was happy to see that he could go back to sleep. I felt guilty about involving him in my craziness to the point of having to wake him from a deep sleep. I went back to bed and slept in fits.

The following day, I saw Jack for our regular session. I told him what had happened the previous night.

"I'm sorry you couldn't reach me," he said. Then, he took out a prescription pad and started writing something on it. *Oh great*, I thought, *he's pushing more pills.*

"Here's my home phone number. Call me if you have a panic attack that won't stop."

I was shocked. Doctors never gave out their personal phone numbers. Patients had several hoops to go through to reach their physicians. In part, this was to protect physicians from excessively needy patients but probably also helped whittle calls down to those that were critical.

Jack saw the surprise on my face. "I don't do this for all patients. I did once have a patient stalk me and had to have a restraining order against her. But I know you won't abuse this."

I thanked him as I took the piece of paper.

"You said you woke Martin up," Jack said. "How did that go?"

"I felt terrible about waking him up. He needs his sleep."

"Hmmm. When your girls are sick or frightened, do they wake you up?"

"Yes, of course."

"So why is it so bad for you to wake Martin?"

"I'm not a child. I shouldn't need to wake him at night to take care of me."

"Oh, so you're a super-human and never need any help?"

I laughed, sort of.

"It's okay to ask for help," Jack said gently. "You're going through a crisis, and Martin wants to help you."

Through my tears, I nodded.

Jack continued. "All your life, you've had to take care of yourself. Your parents weren't there for you when you were a child. Even though you eventually lived with your mother, she wasn't there for you emotionally. So you were forced to fend for yourself. You didn't learn how to express your feelings, your needs. Now, with all that you're trying to do, you have a lot of emotions. Anybody would have those emotions. Anxiety is your mind and body trying to express those emotions. In therapy, we're going to help you find the words to say to let the emotions out. They won't be as painful when you can talk about them."

I must have looked surprised because he continued, "I guarantee that you'll feel better when you are able to say what you feel."

As I drove home, I wondered how he knew I wouldn't abuse this privilege of having his home number. Why did he trust me? What if I turned out to be a stalker? Or what if I annoyed his wife and children with my calls? His family needed him, I knew. He worked the late shift in a crisis center and days in his practice. I couldn't interfere with that sacred family time when he wasn't working. Yet, I felt special, knowing that he wanted to take care of me if I couldn't see my way out of a crisis. I never did call his home number but having it was therapeutic.

Over the next few days, I paid attention to my fears. Maybe that would help me get to the feelings Jack talked about. I forced myself to think about my worries. There were many. If I caught a cold, I expected it to proceed to pneumonia, and I'd die. If I experienced a pain in my body, it meant I had cancer that would kill me. When I came home to an empty house, there would be a bogeyman hiding in a closet; he'd jump out and kill me. An airplane flight would inevitably crash, and I'd die. After taking a doctor-prescribed medicine, I'd experience an unexpected side effect, and succumb. I'd have a rare, fatal reaction to a vaccine. An allergy-inducing food would kill me. A road trip through a mountainous terrain would end up with the car tumbling down a cliff, killing me. I noticed a pattern.

Jack had told me that I had a generalized anxiety disorder and that the panic attacks were part of that. I pictured it like having a chronic medical condition that flared on occasion. Only right now the flares were happening every night. I guessed that was why Jack said I was in a crisis.

Martin attended my next session with Jack. Jack asked Martin if he minded that I'd woken him up during my panic attack.

"No, I didn't mind," Martin said. "I just didn't know what to do."

Jack looked at me and raised his eyebrows. "So, Anne, Martin says he doesn't mind."

"I don't believe him," I mumbled.

Both men smiled. "So he's lying?" Jack asked.

"No, I think he's just being polite."

"Is that true?" Jack asked Martin.

Martin shook his head.

"Why are you so afraid to wake up your husband when you're in crisis?" Jack asked.

I thought for a minute. "My mother would scream and hit me if I woke her. I used to wake her up if I wet the bed when I was little. One time she so was so angry that she rubbed the urine-soaked sheets into my face."

"How does that make you feel now?"

"Really sad," I said with a thick voice. Martin took my hand. That released my tears. We sat quietly for a minute while I cried.

"Martin isn't going to hurt you if you wake him up. You understand that, right?"

I nodded.

"You're an adult now, and your mother can't hurt you anymore. Do you understand that?"

I nodded again.

"Do you think you can trust Martin now to help you?"

Sobbing, I said, "Yes." I was in Martin's arms by now.

Martin remembers things a little differently before he joined me in therapy. Jack had recommended that I watch *The Great Santini*, as a movie that explores complex family relationships. We rented the videotape and watched it together, late, because the girls took forever to get to sleep.

Martin's take-away from the movie was that the rigid, abusive military father was an asshole. He thought Jack had suggested the movie so we could see parallels between the movie's parents and us. He worried that Jack had already decided that Martin was the asshole dad. It was clear to me that Jack thought Martin was pretty cool. He would have written into his notes that a stable, loving husband was one of my assets. "Assets" are good things in psychiatry-speak. Patients with involved family or friends are much more likely to recover from mental illnesses and less likely to have severe or relapsing disease.

While my emotional life was in shambles, my social life was improving. Other students now invited me to some school parties. Most we didn't attend. The effort to get the girls ready for bed, pick up a sitter, and drive down to southern Westchester, seemed too great for the short amount of time we could spend partying. But we did attend a few.

One was held in an upscale cocktail lounge in Tarrytown, New York. I wore a shiny pink satin blouse and skirt, along with black pantyhose and high heels. I didn't look very mom-ish. As soon as we walked in, and I saw the other students, I headed right for the bar. I downed a glass of wine quickly and grabbed another. As if one couldn't just walk around a party with two empty hands. I talked with several groups of students, ones I knew, ones I barely knew. I smiled a lot. I laughed. I was funny. I talked with a cool neurology attending. I was grown-up and sophisticated. I could mingle with real doctors. It was a glorious evening. Martin talked with some of the other students and with the cool neurologist. He nursed one drink all evening.

At one point, I headed to the ladies' room. On the way, I found myself face-to-face with another young woman who stood right in front of me and didn't seem to want to move out of my way. It took me several long seconds to realize that I was standing in front of a mirror and had not recognized myself. I was about as smart as a cat at that moment.

Afterward, I found Martin who had seen my interactions with myself. "You walked into a mirror!" he laughed. Out of the corner of my eye, I saw a student, a know-it-all who answered our teachers' questions before anyone else could answer, scrunch her face at me in disgust.

Back at home, I passed out as soon as I hit the pillow but woke a couple of hours later in a terrible panic attack that lasted for hours. While I didn't drink often during medical school—at home the most I'd have was half a can of beer—at social gatherings I'd drink more. It never worked out well, and now that I had panic attacks, it was treacherous.

Jack explained to me that alcohol is a stimulant as well as a depressant. The first drink or two makes you feel relaxed, and the one or two after that can make you quite drowsy. But after the depressant effects wear off, the stimulating effects kick in. For most people, that stimulating effect might just cause a restless night. For me, it caused intense panic attacks.

"Should I avoid alcohol?" I asked Jack.

"How much are you drinking?"

I explained my pattern. Split a beer with Martin on Friday nights to celebrate the end of the week. No drinking on other nights. Several glasses of wine about once a month at a school party.

"I'm not worried about your drinking," Jack said. "But the more you have, the more likely you will be to experience the stimulating effects of alcohol. Just watch how much you're having."

I had a love-hate relationship with alcohol. Because of it, there were no men in my childhood. My father's drinking caused the break-up of my parent's marriage several months before I was born and was likely one of the reasons he stayed out of my life. My mother's father was a mean drunk, and his bitter anger kept my mother away from him. He died when I was eight years old. My mother and aunt were practically teetotalers. My mother kept a bottle of port deep in a closet that she'd occasionally take a taste of on a cold night. My aunt bought one six-pack of beer each summer. She drank a can each week, accompanied by a jar of pickled pigs' feet.

I heard stories of kids drinking in our high school, but my friends and I did not have access. It wouldn't have occurred to me to drink—I was too afraid of my mother giving me a beating.

It took less than a week away from home in my college dorm for me to down a half bottle of Ripple wine, say things I shouldn't have said, pass out, and wake up dry-mouthed and confused. While a half bottle of wine might be nothing for a serious drinker, for a seventeen-year old alcohol virgin, it was a significant amount, especially drunk fast with no food. I discovered I loved to drink. It eliminated my social inhibitions. My shyness disappeared. I was fun, or at least I thought I was fun. I drank a lot, whenever I could. The only thing that kept me from becoming a constant drunk was that I had very little money. I was a scholarship student, which covered my tuition, room, and board. I had to pay for my books, clothes, and extras. Alcohol would come under the "extras" category. I'd saved money from my summer job, but that had to last me the entire year. I couldn't afford a drinking habit. So, I only drank when alcohol was available for free, usually at keg parties. Often these were at Boston College, a streetcar ride away from my college. Later, we'd discover ladies' nights at the local bars. The cover charges were dropped for girls on those nights, and we'd plan on some guys buying us drinks. I'd drink enough watered-down beer to get a good buzz going but luckily managed to get back to the dorm in one piece.

My love of alcohol continued through college and a couple of years beyond, although my lack of funds still limited my intake. When it was a choice between paying rent, buying food, or buying cheap wine, I chose the rent and food. But if someone offered free booze, I drank. Things changed as soon as I married. I wanted to be a respectable wife. My husband was not much of a drinker, and I was too embarrassed to drink more than he did. Then, a year after we married, I became pregnant. My intake plummeted to zero during pregnancy and breastfeeding. Even after finishing breastfeeding, I drank little. It was impossible to drink when our girls were awake, and one of us usually stayed with them until they fell asleep. The one who did not stay with the girls did the clean-up from supper. Alcohol didn't fit into our lifestyle.

I asked Jack if I should avoid caffeine. After all, coffee makes people jittery, so perhaps that could be causing my panic attacks? Jack just smiled and shook his head. He didn't even ask how much coffee I drank. I asked him if I should change my diet. "Only if you're worried about your cholesterol," he said. Perhaps the anatomy lab chemicals were affecting my brain, I suggested. "The smells are pungent," he said, "but they're not causing your anxiety or panic attacks." Maybe I'm not getting enough sleep, I mused. "I'm sure your sleep is disrupted by your anxiety." He wasn't buying it happening the other way around.

"Your anxiety is coming from the emotions you're holding in."

When I looked skeptical, my usual expression in his office, he suggested that I buy and read *The Road Less Traveled* by M. Scott Peck. I said I had no time to read a book. He then proceeded to explain it to me. Intrigued, I bought it and leafed through it. One sentence caught my eye: "To the child, abandonment by its parents is the equivalent of death." I put the book aside, vowing to return to it during the summer break from classes. In the meantime, I wondered if I'd been trying to live a life while dead inside. Could this doctor breathe life back into me with his therapy? Or would I be prevented from living life fully? Was I like the bodies that surrounded me in the anatomy lab, lying still, shrouded, visionless, dead?

When the heat goes out in your house, you and your loved ones can pile into one bed, cover yourselves with blankets, and sleep. You share the experience of the cold. Cuddling together keeps you warmer and makes the experience bearable. I had largely endured my anxiety and panic attacks alone. Sharing my feelings with Jack, who understood the symptoms, who'd treated other patients with my concerns, helped me feel less isolated. Sharing my feelings with Martin provided the warmth of cuddling.

During quiet times, driving to and from the medical school campus, I thought about what I was going through, about my life, about Martin and the girls, about Jack. I felt like I was spiraling downward, like the feeling I'd had when undergoing general anesthesia at age seven to have my tonsils removed. The doctor had placed an ether-soaked mask over my mouth and nose. My vision had traveled down an inverted cone into blackness.

The sides of my life's cone now were slippery with my emotional limitations, but I was fortunate to have a kind doctor and a loving husband working to prevent my further descent and help me out of the abyss. I just didn't know if they'd be able to succeed.

Chapter 18

I stood at the sliding window that separated the room full of sick kids from a room full of nurses, medical assistants, and administrative staff. I held Cassie in my arms, her head resting on my shoulder as if trying to quell the pain that raged in her ear. Rachel leaned against my hip, her head in a book. The pediatrician walked through the medical staff area and placed a folder in front of the administrator.

"No charge," he said and hurried off to his next patient. I thanked his back and thanked the administrator and thanked the nurse who smiled warmly at Cassie. With a pang of guilt for not paying, I made appointments for Cassie's follow-up and a yearly checkup for Rachel.

While in medical school, I paid very little for healthcare for my family and me. The pediatrician, internist, gynecologist, and eye doctor charged nothing. "Professional courtesy," they called it. I'd protested at first, saying we had insurance and could afford it. Because we saw him so often, Jack did allow us to pay, but at a reduced rate. This generosity of our doctors was part of a tradition in New York. It felt wonderful to be part of this large family that looked out for each other. I knew I'd be expected to do the same when I became a real doctor, a pay-it-forward thing.

In addition to this financial giving, the doctors impressed me with their nurturing care of all of us. My clinical teachers at school also stressed the notion that the patient always comes first, as much as humanly possible. The breast surgeon had surely declined some holiday activity by performing my procedure the day after Christmas.

These doctors cared deeply about the patients they served. I wanted to have that level of dedication. I wanted to help relieve people's suffering. I also wanted to alleviate my family's pain, the pain I'd inflicted on them by asking them to move 3,000 miles so I could pursue a change in career. To do this, I had to do better. I had to recover mentally. I needed to stop dragging my feet about the work in therapy. I would have to admit my limitations and no longer hide behind a screen of shy, awkward, "not emotional." This would require breaking down my barriers to emotions and beginning to feel the feelings. I had to stop fretting about failure and buckle down to study. I would do this for myself, Martin, the girls, Jack, and my future patients.

In retrospect, I can see that Medicine was both an adversary and an aide on my path to becoming a healer. It demanded too much of me—too much time, energy, concentration, and determination. It took me away from my family. It allowed me few hours for other joys—friends, hobbies, self-care, voluntarism. Medicine was a jealous, possessive lover, demanding complete fidelity.

And yet, Medicine was generous to me. It gave me the tools to bring health to others. It gave me the credentials to be seen as an important, contributing member of a community. It gave me the opportunity to learn a vast and fascinating body of knowledge. Medicine taught me the skills to save lives. Its people also took care of my family and me with excellent healthcare at little or no charge.

Airline preflight instructions tell parents that in the event of oxygen masks deploying, they should apply their own masks before that of their children. They say this because parents without oxygen may lose consciousness before they can finish helping their children. Similarly, before I could save others as a doctor, I needed to save myself as a patient.

"Hello, my name is Anne, and I'm not an alcoholic. I'm an imposter, here because my medical school's Behavioral Medicine professor says I have to attend one Alcoholics Anonymous (AA) meeting." Admittedly, I only thought about saying this, but I was indeed at an AA meeting that afternoon. I sat on a rickety folding chair at the back of a church's downstairs community room, sipping bad coffee. No one had removed their coats, I noticed. The room was not chilly; I imagined that the attendees wanted to flee quickly should they not be able to tolerate the hour-long emotional sharing. Part of me wanted to flee also. I worried that someone in this Yorktown Heights meeting would recognize me and assume I was here for the obvious reason.

The Behavioral Medicine course gave us several opportunities to observe people who struggle with mental health issues. We met a hospitalized teenage girl with bipolar disorder, who described her current manic symptoms as like being in a tunnel with traffic whizzing by on both sides of her face. We watched a psychiatrist interview a patient with Korsakoff Syndrome, the result of vitamin B_1 deficiency from longstanding, excessive alcohol use. He sat in a wheelchair, his speech made little sense, and he had little long- and short-term memory. We interviewed a patient with major depression. The attending had told us she was not responding to antidepressant medications. The patient didn't seem to care that she had an audience. In a monotone, she responded to our questions. She made little eye contact. This lack of showing a normal range of feelings is called "flat affect."

These patients' suffering made my anxiety seem like a minor cold in comparison. I'd learned that I was called "highly functional." As in, an individual suffering from a mental disorder but with excellent family, social, and work resources. Such people can manage their symptoms well and live full lives. Most of the patients I would meet in the Behavioral Medicine course and later in psychiatry rotations were on the "low functional" side. Either their lack of family, social, and work resources caused their severe psychological symptoms or the loss of resources was the result of their mental disease. They didn't do very well, on average, and many rotated among hospitals, halfway houses, jails, and the streets.

Because alcohol abuse is so common, our professor said, we students needed to understand its effects on patients. Attending an AA meeting is an excellent way to observe people as they struggle to overcome their addiction, he told us.

I listened to people describe their battles with alcohol and their continued skirmishes and fights to fend off the pervasive temptation to drink. With raspy voices, they described jobs lost, marriages ruined, children who would not talk to them. Their strength inspired me, while at the same time, I wondered what terrible effects their drinking had had on their children, spouses, friends, and coworkers.

My mind drifted to the alcoholics in my family. Had my father ever attended an AA meeting? His alcohol abuse caused him to abandon me, ruined two marriages, cost him jobs, and perhaps led to his decision to cheat on taxes, which led to a stint in prison. But even after I got to know him when I was in my late teens and early twenties, he was drinking steadily and never admitted to having a problem.

AA was primarily used by men at the time when my father's mother, who died shortly after I was born, was downing whatever liquor she could sneak into the apartment on the little household allowance she had. It seemed unlikely that she had help with her addiction. My mother's father drank steadily after his wife died, leaving him with two teenage daughters to raise. He was a marginally functional drunk and kept his job as a tack factory worker until he retired. But I doubt if AA made it down to his rural southeast Massachusetts town in the 1940s and '50s.

The attendees' stories filtered through my reveries. I was impressed with their bravery and honesty. All were attempting to get their lives in order, even if not all would succeed. The long-timers had straightened up themselves by getting in touch with their feelings and admitting they needed help. I realized they were doing what I needed to do. While they had gotten high to avoid their emotions, I had hidden my feelings with avoidance tactics.

The pain on their faces was almost palpable as they confessed their sins. I'd later learn in clinic that alcoholics complain of physical pain "all over, Doc." One of my mentors told me this was because alcohol dulled physical sensations and, when it was removed, alcoholics feel intense pain. Like these recovering alcoholics, by lifting my defenses against emotions, I now felt the pain. I was moving from the "pins and needles" sensation of the panic attacks to the stabbing pain of admitting how I'd avoided deep feelings like love, anger, and sadness.

The next day, I sat again in a folding metal chair. This time, I was with twenty or so students and the same psychiatry professor who had written his number on the blackboard at orientation and who had referred me to Jack. Today we would learn about psychiatric medications. That the professor had opted to arrange our group in a circle was interesting. If he planned to lecture on medications, why didn't he stand at a blackboard? Were we going to discuss these treatments, as if we students could possibly have any opinion? We were not yet licensed to prescribe medicines, so anything we learned was theoretical to us.

The psychiatrist reminded us that his name was Dr. Jones and that he was a professor in the department of psychiatry. He also saw patients with psychiatry residents in the medical school clinic and inpatient service, and he had a private outpatient practice. Dr. Jones described the major classes of drugs: antipsychotics, antidepressants, anxiolytics, mood stabilizers, and depressants. Prior to the mid-1900s, very few drugs were available to treat psychiatric illnesses, and the sickest patients had to be hospitalized and restrained. Now, doctors could treat almost everything in outpatient clinics.

I listened intently to his descriptions of anxiolytic medications, wondering if there were other drugs Jack could have offered me. But my mind wandered as the professor detailed the array of antipsychotic drugs that were used to treat patients with hallucinations. Suddenly, I snapped to attention.

"Some colleagues of mine, also psychiatrists, decided to try several of the treatments that they prescribed for their patients. Many patients won't take their medications because they don't like the way they make them feel. My friends decided to try them for themselves."

All eyes in the room were wide, staring at the professor. Many, I'm sure, had tried illicit drugs. But trying legitimate drugs just to test out how they made you feel?

"Was this legal?" asked one brave student.

The doctor laughed. "Probably. I'm not sure they checked."

"What did they discover?" asked another student.

"Well, the antidepressant, a tricyclic, didn't feel like much of anything. That wasn't a surprise—those drugs take a few weeks to start working. They don't have immediate effects. The benzodiazepines were relaxing and worked pretty quickly, sort of like a nice gentle high."

Aha, I thought. Good thing I'd avoided the benzodiazepine Jack prescribed for me. I couldn't afford to get high.

The professor continued. "Something fascinating happened when they tried Thorazine. This is what we use for schizophrenic patients. These patients often need 200 milligrams or more each day to get their symptoms under control. My friends took just ten milligrams each— the lowest dose. That low dose knocked them both out. They slept for almost two days."

I wondered if Jack was one of these rogue doctors. I could easily see him trying a medicine for the fun of it, with the benefit of understanding what his patients experienced. I wanted to raise my hand to ask if this was the case but didn't dare.

Later, I would learn that Jack was indeed one of the drug-toting doctors. Jack was a free spirit. Sure, he was a doctor, taking care of real patients, but he'd told me he went to medical school to avoid the draft during the Vietnam War. That he kept an office in a dilapidated old house confirmed that he wasn't in the field for the big bucks although he splurged a little on vehicles. In nice weather, he rode a motorcycle. In the winter, he drove a black Chevy Corvette. And, he loved John Lennon—a kindred peaceful spirit until his murder in 1980.

At our next joint Saturday appointment, Jack, Martin, and I talked about rules and rebellions. Martin described our regulation about sweets for the girls. They were allowed a limited amount and only every other day.

"Wow," said Jack. "How do they feel about that?"

"They're nice on the sweets days, but the sugar-free days are hell," Martin replied.

"I'm wondering why you only let them have sweets every other day?" Jack asked.

Neither of us answered at first. I was wondering myself why we had chosen that schedule. Martin finally responded.

"We don't want them to eat too much sugar. It's bad for their health. It's bad for their teeth."

"Doesn't it seem kind of rigid? Is there another way you could help them eat healthy but in a more flexible way?"

"I guess so," Martin said.

"Sure," I said.

"When parents are too rigid, it's kind of hard to keep the emotional connections with their kids. You do have to teach them right from wrong, to guide them along, but I think the key is love, not laws."

Martin and I talked about this on the way home. Martin was more authoritarian than I—he'd been raised by authoritarian parents and had adapted their parenting style. My mother had been domineering, but I'd vowed to never parent the way she did. As a result, I'd followed a more permissive path while the girls were young. Or at least I thought I did. In retrospect, I doubt my assumptions. Perhaps I wanted the black-or-white decisions—I just didn't want to implement them. I let Martin be the enforcer. It was much easier to make him the bad guy and to avoid the gray negotiations that would be needed if we didn't do the black-or-white method of childrearing. This method wasn't fair to any of us.

I hated to see the girls upset and couldn't bear to hear them cry or whine. I liked Jack's sugar approach, and I tentatively suggested that we stop the every-other-day rule. We could still limit how many sweets the girls ate, but perhaps they could have one treat every day. After Martin's mother left that day, we announced the new sugar policy to the girls.

"Yay!!!!" they shouted in unison.

Rachel, always curious, asked why.

Martin explained. "Jack said we were being too rigid. He said we could still encourage you to eat healthy but let you have a treat every day if you want."

"Yay, Jack! Yay, Jack! Yay, Jack!" The girls were jumping up and down during this chant. Pretty soon Martin and I joined in.

Later, in bed, I thought more about this change. I wondered if I was too rigid with myself. I'd decided that if I didn't pass an exam or a course, I was a failed medical student. If I didn't make it through medical school, I had failed as a person. I'd not given myself permission to see that I'd chosen a Herculean task for myself by trying to succeed in Medicine while mothering two young girls. I'd been the authoritarian parent to myself. What I needed to do now was to become the loving, caring parent who guides the child along, applauds her successes, and encourages her when she fails. I needed to be a Good Mother to myself.

I'd suffered from violent and negligent mothering as a child, but as Jack was teaching me, I was an adult and no longer needed to fear my mother. She couldn't hurt me now. I realized that my goals had not changed—I desperately want to be a doctor and wanted to help others. To accomplish that, I needed to overcome the debilitating anxiety and panic attacks. To do this, if Jack was right, I'd need to get in touch with my emotions.

I vowed to pay more attention to how I felt at any particular moment. I vowed to talk about my emotions, to Martin, to Jack, to friends, to myself. I promised myself to stop being my harshest critic. I swore that I'd change my defining four-letter "F" word from "fear" to "feel."

Chapter 19

I had the beginnings of a panic attack a couple of nights before an exam. It started in my legs—the pins and needles feeling. I'd been ruminating on the enormity of material I still had to master in the next couple of days. As the panic threatened to swallow me whole, I remembered Jack's words: "You can do it. You have the ability. You'll make it through this." There were no smartphone panic attack apps in those days. If you were going to use breathing to tame a panic attack, you were on your own. Jack hadn't told me about breathing, but the crisis hotline doctor had explained it to me. I used that technique—slow breath in through my nose, hold it for a couple of counts, slow breath out through my mouth. All while remembering Jack's words, like a mantra. My heart rate slowed, my breathing became more regular, and the pins and needles sensation subsided.

At our session the next day, I told Jack what happened. He explained it as "the voice in your head." I wondered if he'd diagnosed me as having auditory hallucinations, but I didn't dare ask. He might tell me I was becoming schizophrenic.

He continued: "This is what a child carries with her when she is separated from her mother. As she faces something she fears, she 'hears' her mother's voice and it soothes her. It helps her cope with the separation.

Each good interaction with her mother reinforces the child being able to internalize the mother's words."

I listened while playing with my hair. The large oak tree outside Jack's office was in full green now.

"You didn't get enough of these good interactions with your mother. She didn't soothe you at home, and she repeatedly abandoned you. So, you were not able to carry her voice in your head. You had nothing to comfort you in unfamiliar circumstances."

I nodded, taking it all in. I could hold onto the things Jack told me, his reassurances that I'd be okay. I could bring them forward into my consciousness at times of need. It wasn't the soothing voice of a loving mother, and it couldn't work retroactively to my childhood, but it helped me now. Jack gave me a "voice in my head."

"You must have felt very angry when your mother left you," Jack said.

"No, not really," I said. Suddenly uncomfortable, I squirmed a little in my chair.

"It's okay to feel angry," he said. He watched me. It seemed like he wanted me to admit I was angry. Maybe he'd like to see me throw some things around his office, smash a chair through his window.

Jack frequently brought up my anger and each time I denied feeling any. He quietly returned to the subject when I tried to deflect it. It unnerved me; I thought nice girls didn't show their ire. Yet, he often said that the anger I didn't release contributed to my anxiety.

I wasn't trying to be obstructive. Rather, I just didn't feel angry often. The few times that something irritated me, perhaps something Martin said, I'd swallow my feelings. I never yelled or shouted, never said "I'm angry." The girls knew how to push my buttons, but I rarely raised my voice with them.

Clearly, Jack wanted me to feel my anger, but it frightened me. I worried that I'd lose control, that I'd become like a banshee, wailing and shrieking. Or a poltergeist, tormenting everyone in my path.

Jack talked about John Lennon frequently. That day, toward the end of our session, he brought him up.

"John Lennon said that fear and love are our two basic motivators. When we have too much fear, we pull back from life. When we have love, we open ourselves to passion, excitement, and acceptance."

I watched the worn carpet and waited for him to say how this pertained to me. He didn't disappoint.

"As a child, you had too much fear and too little love. It made you pull back into yourself. You didn't feel accepted. You dared not experience excitement or passion—there was too great a chance of those being ripped away from you."

I nodded, not sure what else to do.

"It wasn't fair," Jack said.

I shook my head, tears forming.

"But now you've built a wonderful life for yourself. You have so much love from your husband and daughters. And that love can help reduce your fear."

I felt calmer then than I'd felt in a long time.

A white business-sized envelope addressed to me appeared in my school mailbox. The return address was the Behavioral Medicine program administrator. Inside, a letter instructed me to arrive at the visitor's entrance to the county jail at 9:00 a.m. on the following Monday. The notice stated that I should wear no jewelry, even a wedding band. My clothing must be modest—no V-necks, short skirts, bare arms, or tight pants. I could not wear high heels. Make-up should be minimal.

All valuables must be left at home. I would need a current, valid, government-issued photo ID and my New York Medical College photo ID. My car keys would be kept by security for the duration of my stay. Our attending that day would be a female psychiatrist who cared for inmates. She'd meet us on the inside. A group of six medical students would meet with some of her patients, accompanied by the attending.

I did as instructed and arrived a few minutes early. A couple of other students were already there, wide-eyed and quiet. We sat in a bare room with metal benches lining the walls. At the far end was a steel door with a small window. It looked like we would enter the prison through that door. I felt curious but frightened. I'd only seen jails on TV and in the movies. I'd only been in a police station once—to get some parking tickets "fixed" by a friend of my father's. I hoped my face didn't register guilt as I recalled that possibly less-than-legal activity.

When all six of us were present, and the clock showed 9:00 a.m., the far door opened, and we were ushered into the inner sanctum. There, we surrendered our IDs and car keys, completed some forms (including next-of-kin, which must have been in case we were taken hostage by rioting prisoners), and were frisked (me by a female guard, I think).

We went through a metal detector and gathered on the inside where a burly guard instructed us to keep our eyes and hands to ourselves, not to talk to the inmates, and to stay with him. I wanted to hold his hand, even though he didn't look like the hand-holding type. Our guard led us down several corridors and up two flights of stairs until we arrived at an area with a sign that read, "Mental Health Services." After we were processed through by the guards and medical personnel, we assembled in a hallway off of which were several rooms. The guard told us this was the forensic ward, where inmates stay whose mental illness is severe enough to prevent them from being housed with the regular population. Before we'd had time to scan the area, a young woman with long, black hair greeted us warmly. She wore a shiny silver blouse with plunging neckline, short red skirt, and high-heeled pumps. I wondered how the inmates reacted to her flagrant display of femininity. She must not have received the clothing memo, I thought.

"Hi, I'm Dr. Nelson," she said.

Her warm smile contrasted with the bleakness of the ward. She led us into a conference room off to the side. The room had no windows and nothing to brighten the gunmetal gray walls. A guard came in and stood inside the room. Dr. Nelson ignored him. She talked about the patients we would meet that day. The first was incarcerated for murdering three people. He had been diagnosed with antisocial personality disorder—a psychopath in other words. She would interview him. She instructed us to listen only, not to ask the patient questions, and not to engage with the patient. We were there to observe.

The patient was delivered by yet another guard. His hands were in handcuffs, his legs in irons. He shuffled over to the chair indicated by the guard. His physique was muscular; I'd expected an inpatient to look sickly. On the attending's questioning, the prisoner stated that he had killed three people. He would be in prison for the rest of his life. He said he was very sorry for what he'd done. He spoke in a monotone, his speech seemed memorized. It was as if he knew he should feel remorse and used the right words to convey that feeling but felt nothing. I looked at his eyes as he spoke, wondering if there would be an eye sign to recognize a psychopath. There wasn't. He described how he'd killed his victims. He didn't seem to care what effect it might have on his audience. I realized that the man had no heart. He couldn't feel empathy for another human being.

Besides the shock value, I wondered why the attending had chosen this patient for us to meet. While doctors should have the skills to identify individuals with antisocial personality disorders, such persons rarely seek psychological treatment without a court order. The prevalence of this disorder is higher among drug abusers and in the prison population, so doctors-in-training especially may encounter such patients. After the guards took the patient away, the attending told us she wanted us to see an extreme form of a psychiatric diagnosis. This patient didn't seem particularly bothered by his past actions, although they had landed him in prison for life. The devastation of the antisocial personality disorder was inflicted on his victims and their loved ones. There wasn't a cure for psychopathy, nor were there known ways to prevent this disorder that likely had both genetic and social causes. Her treatment goal for this patient was to control his violent impulses. She kept him heavily medicated and worked with the guards to mete out small rewards for good behavior.

I don't recall the other patients we saw that day. I was very happy to leave that conference room, walk through the halls, go back downstairs, exit through security, return to my car, and drive home. All the while, I thought of the man with no heart.

In my Clinical Medicine class, I interviewed a seventy-year-old gentleman with angina, the chest pain that can result from blocked coronary arteries. He took several medications for his heart disease, and he felt pretty energetic most of the time. He was retired but traveled extensively with his wife, including cross-country trips to visit grandchildren. After I interviewed him and performed a physical exam, I wrote up a history and physical note. Since I was a medical student, the attending expected a discussion of the underlying disease process and the physiological effects of the patients' cardiac medications.

As I wrote my report, I realized that my knowledge of cardiovascular physiology was sketchy. We had studied cardiovascular physiology soon after Christmas, when I was still recovering from my breast surgery, my mother and aunt's visit, the holidays, and the onset of panic attacks. While I'd passed the make-up exam that covered the heart and vascular system, I'd not learned the material well enough for it to be second nature. I had to relearn how the heart works as I wrote up this patient's history and physical report. I recalled learning the anatomy of the heart. It was the afternoon before a practical exam. The anatomy lab was abuzz with students studying their cadavers. I moved around my table to get better views of the cardiovascular system. Suddenly, I stepped on something squishy. I looked down and saw that under my lab shoe was a human heart. I reached down, picked it up with my gloved hand, and held it aloft. I had a perfect three-dimensional view of the organ.

"Hey, that's where that went!" exclaimed a guy from the next table. I handed it over with a smile. I was not the type to step on hearts!

Thinking about the human heart, I wondered if I didn't know my own heart well. I'd spent my life processing thoughts with the parts of my brain that don't deal with emotions. It was time that I opened my heart.

Recently, I served on a committee to help the US government set guidelines for physical activity. The committee worked for two years, reviewed thousands of scientific studies, and wrote an official report. We looked at endurance, the ability to keep exercising over an extended time period. We considered strength, the ability to lift and carry. We studied flexibility, which is important for joints and muscles to be able to stretch without breaking. In the process, we determined that any amount of physical activity is beneficial in reducing risk for heart disease, stroke, cancer, and many other diseases. In other words, every step counts. Back in medical school, with my family, in therapy, in my heart, each small step mattered. The baby steps I took—to identify my emotions, share my thoughts, ask for help, and feel the gratitude—increased my emotional endurance, strength, and flexibility.

Chapter 20

JUNE TO
AUGUST 1986

Freshman year ended. I passed all my courses. I'd now have the summer off. I felt like I'd been released from the county jail that shared the medical school's campus. Although my break was just a two-month furlough, I was giddy with the freedom. I had no plans other than to be a mom and enjoy the summer vacation. If I were a crier outside of therapy, I'd shed tears of joy.

My girls had no problems shedding tears, as they were demonstrating while I drove them to their swimming lessons. I'd signed them up for daily group lessons at the town pool. Today was the first lesson.

"Mom, I hate swimming. Why do we have to go?" Rachel wailed. Cassie repeated Rachel's words and wails.

"Because I want you to learn to swim so you won't drown," I said.

"We won't drown," Rachel argued. "We'll stay away from deep water."

"What if you go in a boat? That's in deep water."

"I get seasick," Rachel countered. "I won't go into a boat."

She had a point there but not enough. "But you've gone in boats with us. You've been on ferries in Seattle. You went in a rowboat on that lake."

"We'll wear life jackets," Cassie piped in. She was now four years old and had added logic to her arguments.

I didn't remind her of the fights we had about using life jackets. "You need to learn how to swim. It's important."

More yowls from the back seat. I tried not to let them tear through my heart. They tolerated the swimming lesson that day, smiled and laughed with the instructor, and showed good progress. But each time I brought them to their lessons, the same scene played out.

While I cried as a young child, as all children do, I was dry-eyed as an older child and teen. I stood out from my peers.

In my inner-city Catholic high school, we had few extracurricular activities. Neither the school nor the parents could afford anything beyond basic textbooks. So when the school arranged for my entire eleventh grade class to attend the movie version of *Romeo and Juliet*, it was unusual and special. One hundred and fifty sixteen-year-old girls and boys, who rarely escaped from their school's brick walls, were bussed to a theater to watch a two-hour movie on teenage love.

We had finished reading the play in our English class the previous month. Seeing the movie was the culmination. Never a Shakespeare fan because I couldn't understand the old English, I managed to slog through *Romeo and Juliet*. I was jealous of Juliet, and wanted someone to fall in love with me, preferably with that much drama. But the double suicide left me cold. I just couldn't understand why these young people would die for love. Still, I was intrigued to see the movie. I rarely saw films—they were too expensive—so this was a treat.

I sat with my friends, a long row of a dozen girls, identical in our forest green school uniforms. Ahead of us sat several of the "cool" girls with their steady boyfriends. I hated that they rested their heads on their boyfriends' shoulders. I wanted a boyfriend's shoulder for myself. One of the girls looked around and smirked, as if to underscore her social success.

The movie followed the play's plot, although the dialogue was much simpler and easier to understand than the original. Even I could follow the plot line. About halfway through, the sound of sniffling filled the theater. Purses were opened, tissues were extracted, noses blown. I realized with a start that people were crying. I wondered what they were crying about. At the end of the movie, the sound of weeping was overpowering. When the lights came on, every girl clutched a tissue, every girl had swollen, red-rimmed eyes, every girl brushed away tears. Every girl but me.

I couldn't figure out what they were crying about. There were gradations to their emotions. Some had wet eyes only. Others had puffy, blinking eyes. Others were weeping quietly. And some were sobbing with gusto. By now, I wanted to sob myself. I wanted to fit in with the group, and if they were all crying, I wanted to cry. I wished I could just turn on a tap.

As a baby in institutions and care homes, I learned not to cry. Later, I learned that kids in orphanages rarely cry—it doesn't do any good— better to save your energy. As an older child, if I failed to stop crying on my mother's demand, she'd slap me until I did stop. As a result of this early imprinting, I cried little as an adult. I wasn't always dry-eyed. A fight with Martin would bring tears, usually when I was alone in bed. I bawled when a school failed to accept one of the girls. I wept when Martin left on business trips when I thought of the possibility that he might not return. But movies and books failed to make me weep. Most funerals left me stone-faced. The exception was for funerals of children. I wept for the little ones, for their parents, for the unfairness of it all.

I told Jack about my inability to cry outside of therapy. At the time, I clutched a wet tissue in my hand—evidence that I might be lying. I continued to be surprised at Jack's ability to turn on my waterworks. It was as if he held the key to a secret lock deep within me.

"It's safe in here, in therapy," Jack explained.

I stared at him.

He continued, "All babies cry, and usually a parent picks them up to soothe them. But when you cried, bad things happened. Your mother sent you away because you cried too much at night. And, equally bad, she told you about this when you were old enough to understand that she didn't want to deal with your tears. Also, she hit you when you cried. No wonder you stopped crying. It wasn't safe."

I nodded, unable to speak, my throat tight.

"You're safe in this office, in therapy. You can feel things in here, and there won't be any negative repercussions. No one is going to tell you it's wrong to cry. You won't be hit. Your crying is you letting out all those feelings, the emotions you've been forced to hold in for all these years."

I soaked a few more tissues at this point. Then I mentioned the girls' tears at going to their swimming lessons.

"Do their tears bother you?" he asked.

"Yes, I guess they do."

"Why?"

I thought for a minute, and then for another minute. "I don't want them to be unhappy."

"Are they happy kids in general?"

"Oh, yes. They are always giggling."

"Maybe they were just anxious about the lessons. Have you asked them why they don't want to go?"

"Yes, but they can't really say why. I suspect Cassie is just mimicking her sister. If her sister loved the lessons, Cassie would, too. Rachel is often anxious about doing new things or doing things she thinks she can't do well."

"Sounds familiar, doesn't it?"

"Huh?"

Jack just smiled and waited.

"Oh, well, I've been anxious about the studying. But I failed two exams—that proves I can't do well."

"That proves a lot of things were going on before those exams—your surgery, the visit from your mother and aunt, the holidays. It doesn't prove that you can't get through medical school. And you're now proving that you can do it by the fact that you've passed everything else."

"I guess you're right," I said quietly. "How can I help them be less afraid of the swimming lessons?" I asked.

"Are you afraid of the water?"

"No, I'm not. I used to love swimming as a kid. It was one of the few sports I did well. I learned at the YMCA day camp."

"Do you get in the water with the girls now?"

"Not so often. I find the water is usually too cold."

"So maybe the girls are copying you. If you swim with them more, they may lose some of their fear."

"I could try that. But their swimming lessons are just for kids, not the moms. We have to stay on the side and watch."

"Why push them to do these group lessons?" Jack asked.

"So they won't drown."

"Maybe they could learn to swim when they're a little older," he countered. "Or you could teach them yourself."

I loved that Jack was all about permissive parenting. But I wasn't happy about having to take on this responsibility. I wanted all to be perfect—the girls would love their lessons, they'd learn to swim, and I wouldn't have to get wet. On the other hand, I hated forcing the girls. I felt cruel, rigid. Looking back, I question why I was so tough on them.

Not much happened that summer. Martin worked. The girls and

I went to lessons (swimming, horseback, gymnastics), played Slip 'N Slide on our lawn, shopped for groceries, had play dates with school friends, and read books under the living room's air conditioner when it got too hot and humid to sit outdoors. The days flew by quickly.

In late August, we spent a week with Martin's family at Garnet Hill Lodge in the Adirondacks. I pictured relaxing on the lakefront beach with a good book, but biting black flies prevented me from reading more than a couple of words at a time. Remembering Jack's suggestion, I ventured into the lake with the girls, testing the waters. I forced myself to submerge into the pain of the cold. It was like the agony of recognizing and relating feelings, followed by the buoyant comfort of letting things go. I let myself relax into the water with the warm sun on my face. The water smelled clean, enriched with energy.

The girls, oblivious to the reasons why Mommy waded into the lake, splashed me and jumped onto me. Where there are children, there is no still water. They enjoyed showing off their water skills—a summer of lessons had made them strong swimmers. I felt proud of all of us.

We visited an old garnet mine that was close to the lodge. We panned for gems. The girls were disappointed not to find treasures in their dirt, but the gift shop souvenirs satisfied them. I thought of how I searched for emotional gems in the massive dirt pile of my psyche.

Chapter 21

Second year came much easier for me, mostly because the material was very interesting. We learned pathology—the study of what can go wrong in the human body, how it happens, and how to recognize it. Early pathologists had helped future generations of medical students by giving names to pathological entities that describe their resemblance to food. There were chocolate cysts—collections of blood and other material found in endometriosis. We learned of *peau d'orange*, the skin puckering seen in inflammatory breast cancer. Strawberry tongue referred to the bright red tongue color in scarlet fever and other illnesses. Berry aneurism was a bulging of arteries in the brain that produces a characteristic shape. Café au lait spots were normal colorations in many people's skin, but too many of them could signal risk for neurofibromatosis. Cherry angiomas were benign bright red spots made up of tiny blood vessels that developed with age in half of adults. Cauliflower-like structures on a heart valve signaled presence of a serious infection. These, and other items named for foods, were far easier to memorize than pathology named after long-dead men. Perhaps it had to do with my lifelong food issues that had caused excessive weight gain alternating with anorexic-like dieting.

The second-year pharmacology course taught us about drugs, the legal kind. Physicians-in-training love drugs, the tools we would use to cure patients. These were the holy waters of modern medicine. In the 1980s, only physicians could prescribe most medications, and few were available over-the-counter. This made doctors the keepers of cures, holders of keys to immortality. Or so we thought. As we became fully trained doctors, we learned the critical importance of listening to patients, making diagnoses, finding out what the patients wanted, and prescribing treatments that fit with patients' life circumstances. Drugs, we would later learn, are not the only or best solution, and more drugs are not always better than fewer drugs. But in second year of medical school, drugs ruled.

In microbiology, we learned about tiny biological things. Under our lab microscopes, they looked beautiful. But we weren't to be deceived by their looks—many of these could be vicious killers.

Clinical Medicine rounded out our class load. I felt more comfortable this year with interviewing patients, asking personal questions, and probing for answers. My physical exam skills were also improving. I learned to differentiate systolic from diastolic heart sounds, to recognize the sounds of liquid in a lung, and how to do a five-minute neurological exam. Although I always introduced myself as a medical student, the patients treated me like a doctor and seemed appreciative of the time and attention I gave them. It was very rewarding and felt like a glimpse into what it would be like to be a real doctor.

I still suffered from panic attacks, but they occurred less frequently and were less powerful. All occurred around exam times.

"I wish you could go to medical school without taking exams," I told Jack.

"Tell me how you feel when you're taking them."

"It's like there is a diabolical creature sitting under the exam, screaming the questions up to me. If I choose the wrong answer, the creature will smile and rub its hands in glee. It wants me to fail."

"You're personifying the exam, as if it's your evil mother out to destroy you."

"Yeah, I guess."

"Maybe you can think of it as more of a game. You've done the reading, now let's see how much you can remember, kind of thing."

I thought of the memory game in which my daughter Cassie routinely bested everyone in the family. If only I had her ability to retain facts, I could think of medical school exams as fun. Lacking that, I'd never enjoy them.

Martin's mother drove her car into the ravine by our driveway that fall, and she didn't know how she got there. Thankfully, the girls were not in the car at the time and Grandma wasn't hurt, but all I could think of was my daughters' safety. I announced that she couldn't drive the girls anymore. Martin didn't contradict me. Grandma thought we were being ridiculous; she felt fine. On our insistence, she saw her doctor and reported back that he said she was fine. Years later, we'd learn that she had long-standing severe aortic stenosis, a narrowing of one of the heart valves that can cause loss of consciousness. To our knowledge, however, she didn't have another serious car event.

She continued to babysit the girls but only at the house. We made sure that the girls had no lessons on Friday afternoons so she only had to oversee their play. Cassie's school provided transportation that year; Grandma just needed to meet the girls at their buses and watch them for the afternoon. I wasn't completely comfortable about the situation but didn't know if I was justified in further restrictions. Besides, Rachel was old enough to use the phone to call for help and neighbors were close by.

With Grandma staying over every Friday night, Martin and I socialized more with friends: medical students, Martin's IBM colleagues, and parents of the girls' friends. I was more relaxed about schoolwork and enjoyed these outings instead of perseverating about lost study time.

I continued to see Jack twice each week—once on my own and once with Martin. It was a slow slog with a lot of repetition. If Jack had a plan for how therapy would proceed, he didn't share it. I didn't understand why it worked, but it felt like a lifeline. That I had to talk in therapy continued to both surprise and annoy me. Before I met Jack, my only knowledge of psychiatric sessions came from the movies. Since an individual session involves a lot of "Tell me how you feel" and crying and "Yeah, I guess," movies just show snippets of sessions. Before I walked into Jack's office the previous year, I'd assumed a psychiatrist would do the talking for me and tell me what to do for my panic attacks. But Jack clearly wanted me to speak my mind. As if I could drag a straight train of thought out of my messy brain. I pictured my neural circuits crisscrossed like a picked-over plate of spaghetti. The pressure to express thoughts and feelings frightened me. Usually no one wanted to hear what I had to say. Why should this doctor be any different? And how was I supposed to make conversation? It wasn't just about weather (always safe). Or about my children (I did love to talk about them—they were so cute and fascinating and loveable). But in a way, Jack's interest in me was refreshing. I began to feel important.

"What if he stops loving me?" I asked Jack one day. He had just encouraged me, again, to talk about my feelings with Martin.

"Why would he stop loving you?"

"If my personality changes, I'll be different. Maybe he won't like the new me."

Jack smiled. "Therapy can't change who you are. It won't change your personality. It can help you think through how to approach things differently. It can help you share what you are feeling. But if you're quiet, it won't make you a talker. If you're boisterous, it won't make you dull."

This disappointed me. I wouldn't mind a personality transplant. I wanted to be the person who attracts friends, the life of the party. But I felt some relief that I wouldn't change so much that I'd turn my husband away. I listened to a U2 tape as I drove home. The title of one song—"I Still Haven't Found What I'm Looking For"—fit my thoughts at that moment. I'd begun therapy to escape from my panic. Now that the attacks were abating, I wanted more from therapy. I wanted to be different and, yet, I was afraid of change.

I sat in classes six hours per day, with information coming at me all of that time. I decided I could spend that time listening closely, memorizing facts as soon as I heard them. It would be a better use of the time than ruminating on how I couldn't do this or that, couldn't learn all the material, couldn't pass the exams. There were no smartphones in those days, no tablets to scroll through during class. A couple of students read the *New York Times* during class, even boldly holding it in front of their faces as if trying to insult the professor. But for me, the only distraction was my own mind. I vowed to pay better attention, study more, worry less.

I also realized that my low self-esteem held me back. Yet I had no excuse for underestimating myself. I had been accepted into medical school—the faculty who'd chosen me must have thought I'd succeed. I decided to listen to Jack and proceed as if I was going to graduate from medical school and become a doctor.

Fake it until you make it became my mantra.

CHAPTER 21

The second-year students produced a musical and theatrical review at the end of the academic year. My friend Kathy created a spoof on the pathology food terms. Several skits poked fun at our professors. Accompanied by a student rock band, I sang with a trio about a bright future. I had hopes that might happen.

Chapter 22

SEPTEMBER
TO OCTOBER 1987

I spent third and fourth year in hospitals and clinics learning how to be a real doctor. I was thrilled—this is the reason I endured the hell of the first two years. I'd rotate among several required clerkships: medicine, surgery, obstetrics/gynecology, psychiatry, neurology, and pediatrics. Later, I would work in a variety of elective clerkships.

Hospitals have a pecking order, and third-year medical students fit right in at the bottom. Above us were the fourth-year students, interns, residents, fellows, and attendings, in that order. Attendings were the fully trained and licensed doctors. They made the final treatment decisions, performed the surgeries, and oversaw the teams of doctors-in-training. They also assigned our grades and wrote our letters of recommendation. The clerkships were taught like apprenticeships. If an intern, resident, fellow, or attending told you to do something, you did it. You followed orders with enthusiasm; a sullen or angry response would earn you demerits on your record. I rather liked the hospital hierarchy. The chain of command was crystal clear. I knew who was my boss. I knew whom to obey without question. I knew whom to fear.

We were there to learn, but our learning was hands-on. We did the scut work—the routine and menial tasks no one else wanted to do. In theory, the interns were responsible for this work, but they delegated as much as possible to medical students. Scut work included such things as drawing blood, taking blood or other tissue samples to the lab for testing, dashing to the lab to pick up results, running to X-ray to obtain readings, and accompanying patients to procedures. In some of the poorer, understaffed hospitals, it could include lifting patients from beds to stretchers, performing electrocardiograms, and bringing bedpans.

In the mornings, we showed up before ward rounds so we could check on our patients and give a report to the team at rounds. The ambitious students arrived an hour early. I arrived only fifteen minutes before rounds. This allowed me to spend time with my daughters before they went to school. We "took call," which meant staying late or overnight at the hospital to take care of patients on the night shift. As students, we only had to do this about once a week.

Like many professions, medicine has uniforms. Medical students wore white jackets. I've since learned that the white coat ceremony tradition began after I finished medical school. The white jacket symbolized belonging. I was now a real medical person. I yearned for the full white coat that I'd wear during residency training, but this first step was meaningful.

If it weren't for the status I donned with the coat, I would not choose white. First, I'm a bit of a slob and regularly spill coffee, tea, and pen ink on white articles of clothing. But those stains can be removed. What I can't erase is the memory of my mother beating me when I was seven years old after I had worn my good white sweater outdoors to play. I could still feel her outrage and the lingering pain where her diamond ring scratched my face. So, it was with mixed feelings that I donned my white jacket.

The white jackets were designed for a different body shape than mine, expecting a doctor-in-training to have wide shoulders and slim hips. My habitus was the exact opposite. I had narrow shoulders—like a cat—and my Irish-peasant hips were built to bear many children. I don't know if I could have purchased a jacket designed for a female body, but I wouldn't have considered it. I wanted the genuine article, the jacket that screamed medical student, even if it made me look like a hot dog spilling out of a bun.

Proudly, I stuffed the jacket's pockets with medical tools—stethoscope, reflex hammer, flashlight, index cards, pens, and a pocket reference. The latter was the medical student's savior, as we could quickly read up on medical tests and normal values, so we wouldn't look so stupid on rounds. On some clerkships, I'd pick up a beeper from the hospital operators so my resident could page me at any time. This too would be stuffed into a pocket.

The medical school provided a name tag that read "Anne McTiernan, Medical Student." I loved that tag—it made me feel official.

Psychiatry, my first clerkship, began with a bang. As I entered the locked psychiatric ward at a community hospital, the door shut behind me loudly as if to announce that leaving would not be easy. I chose to do psychiatry early because I was sure I wanted to become a psychiatrist. Convinced from my two years of therapy that psychiatry was fascinating and rewarding, I decided that this was the field for me. I also thought that my experience as a patient would give me a leg up on other students; I was sure I'd get an excellent recommendation from my clerkship attending. I was an expert, or so I thought. It was like someone who'd had a broken leg figuring she knows all about orthopedics.

A half dozen students were assigned to the same hospital psychiatric ward. I followed signs down pristine white halls to the nursing station where we had been instructed to meet. I avoided making eye contact with anyone. I was afraid the patients would be volatile or that the staff would mistake me for a patient and put me into a locked room. I recognized a couple of fellow medical students standing near a glass-encased nurses' station and walked over to join them. A male in scrubs inside the station opened the door and scolded us.

"You're obstructing the view of the patients. We need to see them at all times. Go sit over there." He pointed at a group of metal chairs that looked like they'd been rescued from a garbage truck. On bad footing already, I thought, hoping the attending hadn't seen this exchange. I was to be disappointed. After six students had assembled, a white-haired woman in a deep purple cardigan and sensible shoes emerged from the fishbowl nurses' station and walked over to us.

"So, you're the students," she said. She didn't sound happy. "C'mon." She led us across to another glass-encased area, this one dark.

"This is my office," she said. "Sit down. It's glass so that I can see what's happening at all times with patients and staff. The glass is dark so that the patients can't see me. You won't believe what can happen on a psych ward."

I wondered which side of the glass I belonged on.

The psychiatrist continued. "This is not your office. You will not hang out here, nor in the nurses' area. You will interview and follow your assigned patients. You will come to ward rounds, which are held every day at 10:00 a.m. Each afternoon, you'll attend a group meeting with one of our attendings."

I sat stunned. I'd expected an attending like Jack. This was not Jack. The attending assigned patients to us. We were to find them (not easy with all the activities that filled the patients' days), interview them, and do a physical exam. Then, we were to write up a full summary of the patient's illness and treatment plan and present to the group.

The next day, one student volunteered to go first.

"What kind of medicine are you thinking of doing, Tom?" the attending asked.

"Cardiology," was the response.

"Great field," she replied, smiling warmly.

Tom presented his patient. "Excellent job," the attending gushed. Tom blushed. We weren't used to effusive praise from our attendings.

My turn came next. The psychiatrist didn't ask what I wanted to be and gave no feedback after I finished. It annoyed me that Tom got the praise. I assumed the favoritism was because he was a male. He wanted to be a cardiologist and didn't need a stellar grade in psychiatry. It didn't occur to me to study how he did his write-up and presentation, that maybe he was just a better student.

That afternoon, we observed a group therapy session led by a different psychiatrist. Afterward, the doctor talked about the patients we had seen. He said that the lack of makeup on one of the patients—a middle-aged woman—was evidence of her deep depression. I rubbed my bare cheeks as I recalled the woman had appeared neatly dressed in pale blue slacks, a striped polo shirt, and sneakers.

"What if she just doesn't like wearing makeup?" I ventured.

The psychiatrist looked at me in disdain. "All Scarsdale housewives wear makeup," he replied. "That she doesn't have any on shows that she doesn't care how she looks. Lack of concern about outward appearance is often a sign of depression."

I didn't live in Scarsdale and wasn't yet middle-aged, but wondered what this doctor thought about my naked face.

Psychiatry smelled like stale cigarettes. Patients could smoke in designated areas of their ward and in the courtyard. They took full advantage of this; most were chain smokers. I ascribed this in part to the boredom of life on a psychiatric ward. It may also have been an attempt to reduce anxiety, as many of the patients had anxious aspects to their various diagnoses. But it was probably mostly due to patients being unable to avoid addictive substances. Tobacco was a legal addiction.

Over the four weeks of the rotation, we met with a young man with narcissistic personality disorder; he was quite impressed with himself and didn't know why he was in the psychiatric ward. We watched our attending interview a teenage girl with borderline personality disorder. Her recent attempted suicide had landed her first in the surgical ward and then the psych ward. After the patient left the interview room, the attending told us the patient had some sort of hair fetish. She explained further that the patient had shaved off all her hair—head and body—right before her suicide attempt. I'd just thought the patient was doing a funky Sinead O'Connor 'do.

I hated the psychiatry rotation. No one seemed happy to be on the ward—not patients, not staff, not doctors. The chief attending was arrogant and uninterested in me as a future doctor. I relayed my dismay to Jack, saying it was the most depressing rotation imaginable. I worried that all my clerkships would be that bad. Jack smiled and said not to worry, that I'd enjoy others. When I said it had ruined my interest in psychiatry, he again said not to worry. He said I'd know by the end of the year what brought me joy. I didn't share his optimism.

As I walked out of the psych ward the last day of my rotation, I noticed the walls were not as pristine as I had thought on my first day. There were stains and scuff marks everywhere.

Chapter 23

OCTOBER TO
DECEMBER 1987

After psychiatry came obstetrics and gynecology. For the three-week obstetrics stint, I was assigned to a South Bronx public hospital that served lower-income patients. On my first call night, a half dozen medical students encircled the chief resident in the hallway of the labor and delivery ward. It was 7:00 p.m.; our shift would end at 7:00 a.m. They went easy on the medical students; the residents worked at least thirty-six hours on their every-third-night call nights. The chief resident instructed us to each take a patient to follow throughout labor and delivery. Slowly, we walked by the rooms, each of which held women or girls lying in beds. Some were accompanied by a man or older-appearing woman. Husband, boyfriend, or mother, I thought. Some labored alone. One by one, the other students selected their "cases." I walked on, not sure whom to choose. All the women were making loud sounds. Did I want a moaner or a screamer? Did I want one with a partner or no helper? Did I want one that looked like a scared child or one who lay back, relaxed, as if this was a vacation from the four preschoolers she had at home?

The darkness of the hallway underscored the poverty of the hospital and patients it served. Perhaps the administrators felt they couldn't pay for illumination, and they justified it by saying the patients didn't realize they could have a better environment for bringing their babies into the world.

Finally, I came upon a quiet room. One bed was unoccupied. A woman slept in the other bed; a man snoozed in the chair beside her. I chose this patient, glad to have some respite from the noise. I read through her chart, sketchy because no doctor or nurse in an inner-city hospital has time to make detailed notes. I learned her name, that she was twenty-one years old, and this was her third child. Twenty minutes later, she woke with a scream. She proceeded to scream every two minutes for the next six hours. Her husband yelled along with her. He bellowed at the nurses to give his wife pain medications. He roared at me to give his wife drugs. He yelled at the chief resident when he popped in quickly to check on the patient. Suddenly, the screams came every minute, at an even higher pitch and intensity. This went on for two hours. I recalled my own two deliveries—in the first I'd labored for almost twenty-four hours, while the second was about six hours long. I may have moaned once or twice but felt embarrassed doing even that. I wished I'd been brave enough to scream.

The chief resident showed up, gloved his hands, and performed a pelvic examination. "Respira, mama," he said and disappeared. The nurse said he'd told the patient to breathe. I realized I'd been holding my own breath. I inhaled then, bringing in the smells of hospital cleaner, rose perfume, the husband's aftershave, and a pungent smell that I'd later learn was amniotic fluid. The smell of that fluid permeated this obstetric ward on which dozens of women labored at any one time.

After an hour, the chief resident returned. Again, he performed an internal exam. "Ten centimeters. Empuje, mama," he shouted as he left. A nurse came in and stood by the patient's bed. "Empuje, mama," she said, repeatedly. Over her shoulder she announced that she was telling the patient to push, that the cervix was fully dilated to ten centimeters. I joined in, not knowing what else to do. The patient began to breathe so fast I thought she was hyperventilating. Her brown cheeks had turned rosy. The nurse walked to the door, stuck her head out, and called for the chief resident. She came back to the bed and said, "Empuje, mama, empuje, mama." The chief resident arrived, examined the patient, and said "Okay, take her down." The husband grumbled that his wife needed drugs. The doctor and nurse ignored him. Later, I'd learn that there were no pain medications available for women in labor in this poor central city hospital. Women who had Cesarean births were given anesthetic to erase the pain. Those in labor did so naturally, not because it was a fad or the healthy thing for their baby but because there was no alternative.

The nurse told me to go with the patient as she helped the mother onto a gurney. The doctor instructed me to scrub up so I could do the delivery. I ran to the sinks outside the delivery room and began to scrub. "Hurry up," shouted the resident as the patient with nurse, husband, and doctor flew past. I ran in, a nurse threw a gown on me, and I struggled into sterile gloves. The resident was right beside me and guided me as I caught the infant that pushed itself out of its screaming mama. The baby, beautiful as all babies are, let out a cry that told me she'd inherited her mama's lungs. As mother and dad cooed over their new little one, the chief resident guided me through cutting the umbilical cord. I congratulated the mother and father on the birth of their beautiful, healthy girl. They smiled but then ignored this unimportant medical student—they knew the teaching hospital pecking order.

I could only touch these newborn infants with medical gloves, but I knew the silken feel of newborn skin from my two daughters and imagined it on these little ones. There was nothing to block the intoxicating smell of a newborn, though.

I marveled at the wonder of childbirth, the introduction of new life into the world. The moms on that ward were poor. Many were young— one was only twelve years old and she was laboring with her second child. Many had limited family to depend upon. But they all loved their babies on sight. I felt honored to witness these momentous life events, while I worried about the hardships both mother and child would face in their depressed environments. They would return to their rat-infested housing projects, bringing their infants home to an area overrun by drug addicts. The moms would have to return to work before being physically ready, and babies would be watched by the cheapest child care providers possible. Hopefully, they would be surrounded by enough love to overcome the fears their environment might engender.

My shift that first night over, I cleaned up, wrote a delivery note, and left the hospital. As I drove home from the depressed South Bronx setting, up past the mansions and rolling hills of Westchester, I thought of how I kept my feelings quiet. I was the sleeping patient. I needed to wake up and scream the feelings, not a real scream but a release of the tension. That would help me give birth to a new life with less anxiety.

For the two remaining weeks on obstetrics, I followed many laboring women and was privileged to deliver their healthy babies. All of the women made noises of some sort as they labored—moans, screams, curses at the men who got them pregnant, calls to their mamas to help them, pleas to God to take away their pain. Whatever method they used, it got them through it. By voicing their pain, they could handle it.

Three weeks of gynecology followed. The senior resident on my team was female, which was rare. Even more rare was that she complimented me on my abilities.

"You have to go into a surgical field," she insisted as she watched me stitch up a patient's skin incision after the attending gynecologist had completed a hysterectomy. I smiled at the praise and told her I'd done a lot of sewing in my life. She looked at me blankly. I realized that most people who end up in medicine spend their time studying rather than doing handicrafts. I grew up in a time when clothing was expensive, in an era before apparel was manufactured cheaply by low-paid workers halfway around the world. As a teenager, I learned to sew because I couldn't afford to buy clothes. Stitching a patient's wound was like hemming a skirt, only skin is much tougher than fabric, you hold the needle with forceps instead of your fingers, and it's best if you get the stitching right the first time. Ripping out a row of sutures to do over was frowned upon.

I also did well with the clinical aspects of gynecology. As a woman, I had little fear of performing pelvic examinations, and the patients seemed to appreciate my concern for their comfort. I enjoyed learning about the many conditions that can affect a woman's female parts and the various methods for treatment. I also noticed that the attendings and residents—female and male—tended to be kind and caring doctors and all appeared to genuinely like women.

I loved the entire obstetrics and gynecology rotation. Unfortunately, the life of an obstetrician or gynecologist would not work for me. It would entail a four-year residency program of early morning rounds, lengthy surgeries, call every third or fourth night, and long days in between. After residency, the schedule would still be overwhelming. Obstetricians need to be available all hours of the day for natural deliveries and emergency Cesarean sections. Gynecologists see their hospital patients before dawn and on weekends. I couldn't see that life fitting for me as a mother. Reluctantly, I crossed OB/GYN off my list of potential specialties.

I watched from the foot of the patient's bed. The surgical intern stood on her right side, and the senior surgical resident stood on her left. It was mid-

December, two weeks into my clerkship in surgery at the county hospital. While it had been a mild start to the winter, I felt cold. I kept my hands in my white jacket pocket to warm them. This rotation was two months long and was the most grueling of the clerkships. My days began with rounding at 6:00 a.m. with the intern who was responsible for up to a dozen patients. Surgical rounds involved reviewing patient charts to learn what had happened during the night, examining the patients, making diagnoses, ordering tests, retrieving results, and ordering medications and procedures. After the intern rounds, we rounded again with the senior resident. During those periods, the intern would present cases to the senior resident, describe the patients' progress, provide relevant test results, and detail proposed treatment plans. We then attended surgical conferences or scrubbed in to observe and assist in operations. Later in the morning, we would round together with the ward attendings, the fully credentialed hospital surgeons who oversaw the wards for a month at a time. Today was Saturday, which meant that after rounds, I'd attend Saturday morning surgical conference at 9:00 a.m. I planned to do my charting after we finished rounds with the senior resident so that I could go home right after the conference.

The intern told the story of the unfortunate patient. She was in her late teens, and two weeks prior had been found unresponsive in her college dormitory room. She had remained comatose during her stay. The cause of her coma had not been determined. Tests of her spinal fluid had ruled out known bacteria and viruses. Her blood had not shown evidence of illegal drugs. Her head CT scan came back normal. Yet, she remained unresponsive, with no sign of recovering consciousness. She was on the neurosurgery service, although no surgery was planned. Because she was under the care of a surgical subspecialty, the surgery residents were required to tend to her. I looked at this young girl, still beautiful even in her deep sleep. Her body was slender, almost child-like. Her skin was alabaster, her hair long and chestnut brown. Its tidiness I ascribed to attentive nurses. There were no relatives in the room, unusual for a critically ill teenager.

"Is she responsive at all?" asked the senior resident.

"No, she doesn't respond to voice, she doesn't move in reaction to noxious stimuli," replied the intern.

"What noxious stimuli do you use?" the senior resident asked.

"I press the supraorbital area," the intern replied and demonstrated the patient's lack of response. This indicated that the patient likely had significant brain damage.

Suddenly, the senior resident pulled up the patient's hospital gown, grasped one of her nipples, and twisted. He repeated the maneuver on the other side.

"Hey, what are you doing?" asked the intern in a whisper.

The resident laughed. "It's a noxious stimulus," he said. He looked at me, smiling. He repeated the maneuvers as he watched my face.

I gave no external reaction. Inside, I was in turmoil. This sick bastard of a resident had just assaulted a patient who could not defend herself. Neither the intern nor I could have done anything to stop it—it had happened so quickly both times. The patient showed no reaction, which also indicated that she was deeply comatose and unable to react. I didn't know if she could feel pain. I hoped she didn't. I felt the pain for her in my breasts.

At the time, I didn't know that nipple twisting was a method of testing comatose patients' levels of consciousness. Even if it was an acceptable means of eliciting pain, there was no excuse for the resident's obvious enjoyment of inflicting pain on a sexual body part and no excuse for taunting the female medical student on the team.

It crossed my mind to report him to the head of the surgical training program. I knew that attending well—he was the doctor who had performed my breast surgery. Just as quickly as I thought of it, however, I dismissed the idea of reporting. On the wards, we learned to go along with what's expected of us, never to complain, to gain the reputation of being agreeable, hardworking clerks. Our grades and recommendation letters depended on this, which would determine what residencies we would be accepted to.

My choice to remain silent was not because of concern about the training program director. He was a wonderful doctor and an excellent mentor. Once, when a few of the female students told him we felt unsafe walking to the student sleeping area because there was no lighting in a hallway, he said he would immediately remedy the situation. He followed through on his promise, and the lighting appeared within a week. There were no repercussions for our stepping up with our concerns. I had no concerns about either the hospital or the medical school. In my experience, both followed high ethical principles for patient care.

Rather, my choice reflected the medical students' perceptions that we had to face adversity on our own without help. Once, the same cruel senior surgical resident had kicked a fellow student as they left the residents' lounge. I whispered to her that she should report him. She disagreed.

"Never complain," she said. "They'll think you're weak."

I'd been told before that I show little emotion. It was like having a poker face but without the game. However, I had higher stakes than money. As a child, an angry look from me would enrage my mother. Screaming, she'd slap my face with vigor, as if to erase my features. It did the trick for her. I learned to compose my features after a slap. I couldn't cry—that would bring another beating. I softened my features, kept my eyebrows, eyes, mouth, and jaw loose, almost slack. I'd learn in medical school to call this look a "blunted affect" or a "flat affect," although it usually refers to a patient's difficulty in feeling and expressing emotions. After a while, I learned to stifle the angry looks and, eventually, I buried the anger so deep I couldn't feel it. All that I felt, it seemed, was fear. And the fear was suffocating me. Jack was teaching me to feel my emotions again. But in a situation like this—where an angry look or action toward a senior resident could get me a poor review on my surgery rotation—I reverted to my flat affect. The surgical mask I wore in the operating suite protected patients against my germs; my flat affect was like a mask to protect me against a vindictive resident.

As I gazed at the senior resident that Saturday morning, I thought of my gentle and strong husband who would never hurt another human being. He wasn't in a healing field, but he knew that protecting people weaker than you was the right thing to do. I thought of my little girls and shuddered at the thought that some monster might someday treat them the way this resident treated this young girl. I longed to be back home with my family, to be surrounded by love rather than cruelty and sadism.

I never learned what happened to that patient. She was transferred off our service. Perhaps she went to a long-term facility for comatose patients. I feared that there would be no happily ever after for that sleeping beauty.

During the surgical conference that morning, my mind wandered off abdominal surgery procedures and onto my family. I realized that rather than being a source of the anxiety I'd been suffering, my family was the antidote. My husband and daughters were my refuge.

Chapter 24

DECEMBER 1987
TO JUNE 1988

The surgery rotation included several one-week mini-rotations. I experienced a week of general surgery where I scrubbed in on an operation to remove an older man's infarcted bowel. The smell was so rancid that the nurses smeared a menthol ointment on our masks to hide it. It didn't work. The week on urology consisted of sitting long hours in a lounge area while the residents were between surgeries. One day a pharmaceutical representative brought Chinese food for lunch. One resident ate out of a plastic vomit basin that he claimed was brand new, never used, and therefore clean. Again, I employed my mask face rather than show my disgust.

I was assigned to a one-week stint in the surgical emergency room of a South Bronx hospital. My shift ran from 6:00 a.m. to 10:00 p.m., Monday through Friday. I would not see the girls that week, but I was grateful that it would only be for five days.

After parking at the hospital that first morning, I sprinted from the deserted parking lot to the emergency room and walked into chaos. Every seat in a large waiting room was filled. Blood seeped through dirty bandages wrapped around hands. Several people held ice to their heads.

Some cradled arms, others extended injured legs. The metallic smell of blood dominated the area. I walked to the nurses' station to announce that I was a medical student assigned to the service. The receptionist pointed to a young man wearing a short white jacket. He turned out to be a fourth-year student, and since the residents were too busy taking care of gunshot wounds, he would be mentoring me that week. He told me to look at the list of patients waiting to be seen, find the first one who needed stitching, bring him or her back to a procedure area, and get a suturing kit from the supply room. Then I should come find him and he'll watch me suture. I followed his instructions. After I infiltrated a local anesthetic and placed a few sutures, the fourth-year student said I was doing fine and left me to continue on my own. For the next sixteen hours, I stitched wounds on hands, arms, legs, and feet. I stitched shoulders and backs. I was told to leave faces to the residents because they knew how to place sutures to reduce scarring. I stopped sewing only long enough to go to the bathroom and grab drinks of water. I ate nothing all day. Sounds drifted to where I toiled: doctors paged, emergency codes called, sirens blared, patients complained. At ten o'clock, I checked out and looked for a security guard to walk me to the parking lot. Finding none, I asked the desk clerk how I should get to my car. "Walk," she said. The fourth-year medical student overheard me and said he could walk me out. "But just this once," he said. "I'm working the all-night shift and can't take time out every night." I asked him if there was some other way to safely get to and from the parking lot, and he said no.

As I drove home, I fretted about the risk to me versus the requirement to show up every day as assigned. I realized that no one other than the fourth-year student had noticed my presence and figured no one would notice my absence. I didn't mind working really hard in medical school and tolerated the lack of sleep, but I couldn't put myself at risk of rape or mugging or worse in the high-risk South Bronx. As a woman, I was accustomed to being more careful because of risk of assault. When driving alone at night, I jumped into my car quickly and immediately locked all doors. I didn't walk alone at night or in deserted areas. At home, I checked doors and windows and wished we had the money for an alarm system. At the ring of the doorbell, I stood on tiptoe to see through the viewfinder before opening the door.

I decided to play hooky and did not return for the rest of the week. This was very unusual for me—I was always the good girl who obeyed the rules. But my daughters needed their mom, and my husband needed his wife.

I thought about the women who lived in the South Bronx. They couldn't play hooky from their environment. They took risks with their lives every day and many suffered from the violent acts I could so easily avoid. I was a privileged white woman learning to be a privileged white doctor.

"If anyone ever asks, you don't have to tell them that you've been in therapy," Jack said.

"Okay," I said, not knowing where this was going.

"Medical boards and hospitals sometimes ask if you've had psychiatric conditions that could interfere with your ability to take care of patients. Your anxiety will not have any effect on your work as a doctor. You're not impaired in any way. So, if you're asked this, just say 'no.' Your therapy is your own personal business."

I nodded, still not really understanding what he meant. I'd learn later that state medical boards asked invasive questions of doctors seeking licenses to practice. More than a third of the states ask if the applicants ever had mental health issues in their entire lifetimes. In many cases, this information is used to deny or retract a physician's license. As a result, physicians have been very reluctant to seek care for psychiatric conditions so they don't have to lie when asked. Or, if they seek care, they may do so in another city or pay out-of-pocket to avoid a record that a medical board or hospital could access. Many doctors self-medicate for their mental health symptoms, an unsafe practice. The lack of mental healthcare is particularly dangerous for physicians who struggle with depression and likely contributes to the high rate of completed suicide in doctors. Female physicians are more than twice as likely to commit suicide than women from the general population. The risk in male doctors is higher than in other men, but the difference is not as great as in women.

I made a mental note of this for the eventual time when I'd be asked these questions. I was relieved that I had not shared my diagnoses or treatments with anyone at my medical school or the hospitals at which I trained. Only the one psychiatrist who had referred me to Jack had knowledge of my call for help and he didn't have access to Jack's records. My case was sealed and secret.

Without being able to share my condition and need for treatment with the clerkship directors at my school and hospitals, it was difficult to arrange sessions with Jack. There was no possibility of telling my resident or attending that I'd need to leave early for weekly medical appointments. Any doctor would realize I was most likely under psychiatric care because few other medical conditions require weekly visits in a young, healthy woman. Jack graciously allowed me to come in the evening after the girls were in bed. He had several working patients for whom he held late sessions, so he was accustomed to meeting this need. Still, I was grateful.

As if one body, the neurology team walked into the patient's room. She sat in a chair, tiny as a doll, wisps of white hair sticking out around her head. She smiled warmly as we approached. I stood closest to her, and leaned down to say, "Good morning, Mrs. Stevens." I noticed her hands. They were long and thin and covered in feces.

"Good morning, dear," she said. "You're new here aren't you?" While it didn't bother me that a patient failed to remember me—I had spent a half hour interviewing her and had left her room an hour ago—this told me something about her state of cognition. The poop on her hands told me something else about her thinking.

The attending had crossed the room by now and stretched out his arm for his usual friendly greeting. Before I had a chance to say anything, they were shaking hands like old friends. He asked her how she was doing. "Fine, sir" she said. He asked what day it was. "It's my birthday," she responded. (It was February 8. Her chart said her date of birth was in September). He asked where we were right then. "We're in that nice place," she answered. The attending said goodbye and led his flock out of the room. Once we were gathered around, he asked us why he had asked those particular questions. Before I had a chance to think, another student—there was always one in the group—blurted out that he was assessing the patient's orientation to name, time, and place.

"Excellent," said the attending. "Mrs. Stevens has dementia, most likely Alzheimer's. Patients like this tend to know their name so I don't always ask that question. But she clearly doesn't know the date or where she is."

I desperately wanted to tell the attending that it would be prudent to clean his hands but didn't want to ruin his teaching stride. I wondered what microbes he might have picked up from the patient and to whom he would transmit an infectious disease during the rest of rounds. I was relieved when he washed his hands in the next patient's room before approaching her bed. I wondered how "feces on hands" would be coded on the Mini-Mental exam that we learned to perform on our neurology patients to assess their cognitive status. Despite his lack of observing brown gunk on pale hands, the attending was an excellent teacher. In the doctors' lounge, he depicted specific neurological deficits by acting out what happens when a piece of brain or nerve fails to function. On the wards, he asked patients to show us specific movements so we could observe. No amount of book-learning could imprint this knowledge as well as this clinical teaching.

The four-week neurology clerkship taught me the power of the brain and nervous system, the devastation that can be wrought when they malfunction, and the ability of many patients to adapt to their conditions. It also taught me the importance of healthy lifestyles early in life to help prevent such illnesses as strokes, multi-infarct dementia, and alcohol-induced brain damage. Neurology wasn't for me, though. I didn't feel smart enough to fully understand the various neurological pathways and felt frustrated about the lack of cures at that time for many of the diseases we saw on the neurology ward.

My internal medicine rotation was at the county medical center. The patients were sicker than those in my surgery and obstetrics rotations—they tended to be older with multiple diseases. I loved the variety of types of diseases I was able to learn about from the patients, however. There was the dentist who contracted hepatitis B before medical workers wore protective gloves. There were the little old ladies with congestive heart failure in for "tune-ups," meaning admitted to relieve some of the excess fluid around their lungs that made it difficult to breathe. There was the young woman dying of alcoholic liver disease. I learned that the adverse effects of alcohol happen at lower doses in women than in men. There were the patients with diabetes, hypertension, and heart disease—a typical trifecta because diabetes damages the heart, vascular system, and kidneys. There was the middle-aged executive who had suffered a cardiac arrest. Without oxygen getting to his brain before he was resuscitated, he had lost critical brain function. He would not likely be able to regain the level of cognition needed to return to his job. There were the young men dying of AIDS in the days before lifesaving HIV treatments were available.

On this rotation, I learned to listen and filter hospital noise at the same time. The public address system worked overtime, paging, announcing, calling, crackling. I learned to ignore most of it but to pay attention when doctors were paged STAT and when codes were called. A code was called if a patient had a cardiac arrest or other severe event. A code was called for out-of-control or violent patients or visitors. Each type of event had its own code. Some were color codes, others were numbered, and there was even a fictitious doctor name or two that referred to a psychiatric emergency. While a third-year medical student was not a critical member of a code team, our medicine attendings wanted us to watch and learn how to resuscitate patients in cardiac arrest. I ran when I heard the words "Code Blue."

My resident and attending were both bright, supportive men. The resident was enthusiastic and treated me as a potential colleague. He treated the patients with respect and caring. The attending first complimented me on my patient write-up and then pointed out a few areas where I could improve. I was so happy to receive the positive feedback that I could have handled hearing about even more shortcomings. I vowed to teach medical students this way when I graduated to a residency program. I'm not sure I was able to fulfill that promise completely, but it helped to have these positive role models to emulate.

Despite the sorry conditions of many of our patients, I looked forward to every day on the medicine ward. It didn't take long to realize that I wanted to be like the wonderful doctors who took care of these sickest patients and helped most of them recover to return home and enjoy life. I decided to apply for internal medicine residencies. This would require another three years of training, but completion of a residency is required to practice medicine in this country. I wanted to be a real doctor.

Martin and I hoped to return to Seattle after I finished medical school. There were limited options for internal medicine residency in Seattle, however. To maximize the odds, I arranged to do a summer clerkship in Seattle between third and fourth years. The only clerkship open to me was a four-week rotation on the bone marrow transplant service at the Fred Hutchinson Cancer Research Center. I'd be back at my former institution but would be working with patients instead of data. Martin organized a summer of research in his old department at the University of Washington, and we signed up the girls for day camp. We arranged to house-sit for one of the university professors who was on sabbatical. All four of us were excited to return to Seattle for the summer.

There was just one problem. I worried about the effects of missing two months of therapy. Jack knew about our plans—he'd encouraged me over the past year to reach for whatever I wanted to do in medicine. He had faith in my abilities to deal with my insecurities and anxieties and to be a successful doctor. This would be a first step toward our dream of once again living in Seattle.

"You'll do fine," Jack reassured me. It was a week before my family and I would fly to the Pacific Northwest. Martin and I would see Jack one more time before we left.

"But what if I start having panic attacks again?"

"You haven't had any in the past year, have you?"

I shook my head. My eyes were getting misty.

"Everything will be okay. You're ready for the change. You've done a lot of hard work and made important changes. And if you do get an attack, you can call me or you can call a crisis line in Seattle. You can always get help."

I swallowed, and then said, "And if this clerkship goes well, and the University of Washington accepts me into their residency program, then we'll move to Seattle for good." I didn't say the unthinkable—that I'd never see him again. I wiped tears from my cheeks.

Jack smiled again. "When we lose someone, whether it's because of a separation like that or even because of a death, a part of them stays with us."

I nodded, understanding a little, wanting to believe.

Chapter 25

JUNE 1988

Everything was settled; our flights were arranged, our living arrangements finalized. We'd fly the next day, on June 26—our twelfth anniversary. We'd drive from the Seattle airport to the coast of Oregon for a week's vacation in Cannon Beach. I'd begin my rotation on July 5, the same day the girls would begin camp.

I mulled this over as Martin and I drove to Jack's on Saturday morning for our couples' therapy session. As much as I looked forward to our summer in Seattle, I dreaded the stretch without seeing Jack. I'd grown to depend on my weekly individual and couples' therapy sessions. They affirmed me, kept me going. Jack had helped me see what I should have seen all along—that I had skills, would become a caring doctor, and had a wonderful, loving family. Furthermore, I now understood that my childhood had been fraught with terror and that my parents had abandoned and abused me. While I accepted these as facts, it was really nice to hear Jack say the words every week: *You'll be okay, you can do it, it's not your fault.*

Also, because I was a multitasker even in those days before technology made everyone a multitasker, I mentally listed the things still to be done for the trip. The goal was to get to bed at some time that night. A cab would pick us up at 8:00 a.m., not too early, but getting two children as well as ourselves organized would be a challenge. Already taken care of: mail and newspapers held, laundry done, refrigerator emptied of perishables. Still to be accomplished for the girls: books to last until we could visit a library, toys minimized to essentials, suitcases packed, stuffed animals selected, and snacks packed for the plane. Martin and I still had to pack our suitcases. His would be easy—he'd count out the number of days likely to elapse between laundries and pack exactly that number of items needed. Mine would take more time, with outfits to match and difficult shoe decisions to make. We had the whole afternoon to finish up—we were in good shape.

I prattled on a bit about the details. Martin didn't mind my lists, but he was usually several steps ahead of me when it came to organization. He had already packed items I would never consider: maps of Seattle, Washington state, and Oregon, paperwork for the rental car we'd pick up at the Seattle airport and for our Cannon Beach hotel, and directions to the faculty member's house where we'd stay after our vacation.

We arrived at Jack's and continued our trip-planning discussion as we walked from the parking area toward his office. As we approached, I saw a small piece of paper tacked to the door. "Due to a family emergency, Dr. Shapiro will not see patients today," it said. Below that was the name and number of a crisis center for any patients who had emergent needs. I burst into tears, surprising myself and Martin with my response. I had been hoping for some words of reassurance from Jack that I'd be okay without therapy over the summer. And now there was no hope of that comfort—I'd have to leave without seeing him. This was the first time Jack had canceled on me. I'd come to rely on his steadfast force in my life. While he wasn't a day-to-day presence like my husband and girls and I never contacted him between sessions, the therapy days anchored me for the rest of the week. They calmed me.

I sniffled on the way home, wondering why Jack had canceled. After a few minutes of selfishness, I worried about what kind of emergency could have happened. It must be serious—Jack was dedicated to his patients. Even in inclement weather, he made his way to his office.

"Well, this gives us more time to get ready," Martin offered.

"I guess," I said.

The girls were surprised to see us early and a little disappointed because their favorite sitter would not get through her usual litany of stories. We took the opportunity to have her stay, which would give us unfettered time to pack. About an hour after we arrived home, the phone rang.

"Is this Anne?" a familiar-sounding voice said. "This is Dr. Jones, from New York Medical."

Remembering that he was a faculty member in the psychiatry department, I wondered briefly what trouble I was in at the school. Dr. Jones continued quickly.

"I'm afraid I have terrible news about Dr. Shapiro. He was killed yesterday in a motorcycle accident."

I slumped to the floor as I yelled, "Noooooo." The doctor was talking, but I couldn't hear his words. I called for Martin. He didn't come quickly enough. When he finally appeared from the basement, I told him what the call was for and gave him the phone. I could hear him talk while I curled myself into a ball. Suddenly Martin was right next to me, handing me the receiver. I put it to my ear.

"Anne are you okay?" Dr. Jones asked. I shook my head.

"Anne, can you say something?"

"I'm here," I said in a very tiny voice.

"Anne, I'm so sorry that this happened to you. You will deal with this and will feel better eventually, but I know it's really hard and shocking to you right now."

I nodded, then remembered to talk. "Okay," I mumbled.

"There's a funeral tomorrow. Why don't you get a pen and paper and I'll give you the information. I'll also give you my phone number if you want to talk to someone." I did as he said, returned to the call, and wrote down the name of the funeral home, time of the service, and his phone number. My script was large and shaky.

"There's also a gathering at his house afterward for family and friends. Since you're a medical student, it will be fine for you and Martin to come."

The line was quiet for a bit, then he continued.

"Jack was a close friend of mine, so I'm having trouble with this right now, too." His voice broke. "But his wife and I thought that it would be good for me to take on some of Jack's patients. So you could think about it, and Martin, too. If you want I'd be happy to see you, at least for the time being until you decide what you want to do."

I thanked him, and we hung up. Afterward, I wished I'd said I was sorry for his loss, but I was too swamped with darkness and despair to think of other people's pain.

The girls appeared, attracted by their mom's wails. I told them about Jack. "Poor Mommy," they said and hugged me tightly. I took some big breaths, hugged them back, and began to get my mind under some sort of control. I couldn't be in a pit of darkness and mother at the same time. I'd have to save the despair for quiet moments.

We decided to go to the funeral. I didn't feel like we would belong there—after all, we were just patients, not family, not friends. But I wanted to say goodbye. We changed our flights to leave one day later and arranged a sitter for the girls.

The funeral was so crowded that we could barely see the rabbi and couldn't hear any of the service. Peering over shoulders, I saw a plain wooden casket with a single red rose on top. This contrasted with the

Irish Catholic funerals in which satin-lined caskets, open to show the made-up deceased, were surrounded by floral displays with cloying scents. This funeral smelled of sweat and tears.

A lot of people loved Jack, as evidenced by the crowds. I wasn't surprised. There were many children and young teens, probably friends of his three children. There were young adults, middle-aged adults, and older persons, likely relatives and friends. Sobbing and nose-blowing punctuated the muted sounds of the service.

The gathering at his house was strange. We knew no one other than Dr. Jones; he kindly talked with us for a while. Martin and I ate a little food and hung around awkwardly. No one mentioned John Lennon. Someone talked about Jack's love of wind chimes and pointed out the numerous versions hanging inside and outdoors. I wondered where Jack had found them. He once told me that he and his wife traveled before having children. I pictured him choosing a wind chime in a hilltop Tuscan flea market. Perhaps friends gifted him with unique ones they discovered when visiting other countries. Maybe his children made some in school. I noticed the details of the wind chimes in a vain attempt to avoid feeling the sorrow that filled that house.

I suspected we were the only patients at the gathering. I watched his wife a little, now his widow. She looked small, overwhelmed. I felt so sorry for her. I couldn't look long at their three children who huddled with her. I didn't want to intrude on their privacy and couldn't deal with the pain in their eyes. We left after less than a half hour.

I cried on the flight out to Seattle. Somehow the crew knew that we had just had an anniversary and gave us a bottle of champagne. I wondered what they thought of a young woman who cried on her anniversary. I cried on the four-hour drive to Cannon Beach. I cried as we explored tide pools in the misty Northwest air, my tears mixing with the salt of the ocean. I cried over our dinner of steamed crab, sourdough bread, and salad. I cried at night in bed all that week. When the vacation was over, and we drove to Seattle to start our summer adventures, I dried my tears, took deep breaths, and smiled.

Jack would have been proud of my tears outside of therapy.

Jack opened my mind and heart to feelings. He helped me have empathy for the little girl in me, the one whose parents abandoned her, the one whose mother hit and belittled her. He taught me that our childhoods affect us lifelong, and how important it is to parent well. He helped me understand how to be a better mother.

In doing all of this, he taught me how a real doctor heals.

Chapter 26

JULY 1988
TO MARCH 1989

On the bone marrow transplant service that summer, I witnessed the hell that human bodies could sink into and the height to which human resilience could reach. Most of our patients had leukemia, a condition in which a rogue white blood cell reproduces rampantly and prevents normal cells from doing their jobs. Doctors at the Fred Hutchinson Cancer Research Center had invented and tested bone marrow transplant to treat this terrible disease. The patients would have died without the treatment and many died in spite of it. Still, the doctors, nurses, and patients themselves never gave up hope. Many clinical trials tested various protocols, to determine the best possible treatments.

In 1988, bone marrow treatment was still in its infancy. All of the patients were young—at that time, doctors didn't think middle-aged or older patients could survive the rigors of the therapies. The patients entered the hospital and expected to stay for at least a month. Some survived to go home and lead normal lives. Some survived but with lifelong health problems from the treatments. Sadly, some didn't make it.

The patients were so sick and the treatments were so specialized that as a medical student I could only observe. The risk of infection was high for all of the patients, so only one or two doctors were allowed to examine the patients. There was no scut work—all tasks were done by specialized personnel. But I didn't need to listen to patients' hearts to see how brave they were to face their serious disease and grueling treatments. I didn't need to palpate their stomachs to understand the nonstop nausea they experienced. I didn't need to conduct a neurological test to observe the havoc the treatments played with the patients' brains and psychology.

The oncologists at the Fred Hutchinson were the most dedicated attendings I had ever met. Twice each day, they met as a group with the fellows and residents and reviewed the progress of each hospitalized patient. All of the doctors knew each patient's history and treatment in detail. That way, when they covered the service, they could provide knowledgeable care for every patient.

I remember the young mother whose transplant didn't take. Her small children came to visit and climbed into bed with her. She looked too exhausted to enjoy their closeness. There was the young man who bled from every possible surface. There was the patient whose lungs failed and deteriorated further even after being put on a ventilator. There was the teenage boy who experienced multiple adverse effects of the treatments and still his leukemia advanced. The young physician who cared for him cried as she reported his death on morning rounds.

After the month on this service, I knew that I could not face the continued sadness that oncologists dealt with daily. Instead, I resolved to help people avoid the cancers that were preventable. I planned to do that by being a primary care physician.

We returned to New York for my last required rotation—pediatrics—in August 1988. My first patient was a five-year-old boy who was in the hospital for a chronic condition. Stuck on our ward for weeks, he required frequent blood tests. The intern sent me in to draw his blood but warned me that this little boy often refused to let the nurses, doctors, or technicians near him. I took a deep breath and entered his room.

"Hi, my name is Anne. I'm a medical student. I'm here to help take care of you."

He said nothing. He looked away and played with a balding teddy bear.

"What's your bear's name?" I asked.

"Teddy," he replied.

"He's cute," I said. That brought a tiny smile.

"I have two little girls," I said. "One of them is five years old, just like you. Her name is Cassie. She has a stuffed seal that she sleeps with and takes everywhere with her."

"What's its name?" he asked.

"Sealie." He smiled.

"Does anything hurt you right now?" I asked.

He shook his head.

"I have to draw some blood today," I said. "I know you sometimes don't like that."

He curled his body away from me.

"Why don't you decide where I can draw the blood from."

He looked at me, eyes wide. Perhaps no one had given him an option before. He pointed to the antecubital vein inside his right elbow.

"Okay, I'll do it there, as quick and gentle as I can."

The gods were kind to me that day. It took less than a minute to do the deed and get the sample. I asked him if he'd like to put the bandage on the area himself. He did. Then I asked if he'd like a bandage for Teddy. He put that one on also.

"You did a great job with that bandage! You could be a doctor or nurse when you grow up."

He nodded and smiled.

"I'll see you tomorrow," I said.

"Bye," he said.

As a mom, I had an advantage in pediatrics. I understood little kids. In most children, emotions were always just under the surface, ready to bounce up and out at the slightest provocation. They laughed when they felt good and cried when they were unhappy. They didn't hide their feelings, unless, as was the case with me, they were subject to abuse or trauma. I observed children who dealt resiliently with the ordeal of a hospital stay. Unfortunately, the sickest kids, the ones who weren't well enough to be discharged, had to deal with the trauma of hospitalization as well as the pain of their illness.

Being a mom also gave me a disadvantage—I empathized too well with the moms. I felt their pain but realized I had no right to. There was the mother of a young teenager dying of leukemia. She stood sentry in her son's room and restricted who could approach his bed. She allowed only certain nurses near his intravenous lines, as she feared her immune-compromised son would develop an infection. We honored her wishes because it was the only thing we could do. I wished I could miraculously cure her precious son.

There were the kids admitted with sickle cell anemia crises. They entered the ward in excruciating pain but left smiling after receiving fluids and pain medications. There were the neonatal ICU babies, so tiny and fragile that we students were not allowed to touch them. There was the four-year-old girl whose seatbelt had crushed her larynx and afterward talked like a cartoon character. There was the baby with Down syndrome who had low muscle tone and cardiac anomalies—she had been admitted for surgery for her heart problems. She reminded me of the little boy with Down syndrome who had been my best friend at the care home I'd lived in when I was a toddler. He was the only other mobile child at that home; all of the other children were so sick they were confined to cribs.

Every one of these children had parents in crisis. Typically, the mom slept in the room with the child. Often a parent was in the room when we did our rounds. Many had other children at home, and many had to work to pay bills. I could see that the disruption to family life would be very challenging, on top of the horror of watching your child suffer.

I did well in pediatrics and functioned as an intern because the service was short on staff. I knew I could not deal long-term with children's suffering, however. The experience made me appreciate the dedicated doctors, nurses, and other medical staff who take care of these most vulnerable patients.

Therapy with Dr. Jones was helpful. The structure was the same as with Jack. I talked about what was bothering me; he helped me think through the roots of my angst. We spent a lot of time talking about Jack. I think it helped him as well as me. He told me some of the specifics about Jack's accident. Perhaps he wanted to unburden himself or he thought I'd be interested since I was almost a doctor. But the exact way that Jack died didn't help me. He was gone. Period. Just when I had created a bond with a father figure, he disappeared from my life, as my own father had done.

Recently, when rummaging through a drawer, I found a newspaper clipping from 1988 with an article about Jack's death. The article details the accident, Jack's life history, his surviving relatives, and information about the funeral. Perhaps saving the article gave me a permanent reminder of him. I also found a photograph of Jack. It must have been available at the funeral or perhaps Dr. Jones gave it to me. I was surprised to see it—I doubt if many people had photos of their therapists in those pre-internet days. It's not like you'd stop a session to say, "Cheese!" and snap a polaroid. The picture shows a smiling man with his shirt sleeves rolled up, and chin resting on his hand as if listening intently. This is exactly how I remember him.

Some patients unfortunately suffer the sudden loss of a therapist. The internet is full of advice and stories of other patients' experiences. In 1988, there was no such means of sharing grief with other patients, however. Martin, Dr. Jones, and I all knew and loved Jack, so were able to process feelings together. But there was no bringing him back.

Dr. Jones mentioned that he felt angry with Jack for his death, which he explained is a normal reaction. I hadn't felt angry, but I did feel annoyed that he'd chosen to ride a motorcycle. As a physician, he should have known of the dangers. Motorcyclists are much more likely to die in an accident than automobile drivers. Maybe my annoyance was me feeling a little anger. Almost a therapeutic breakthrough.

Dr. Jones was big into dreams. On his suggestion that I write them down as soon as I woke, I began to remember them. Often, I'd begin a session recounting a recent dream. Dr. Jones told me I had very interesting dreams. I beamed inside, like a star student. Only in this case I was a star psychotherapy patient. In many of my dreams, I had another baby, and I was neglecting it. Dr. Jones suggested that I was the baby—with the time and effort I put into worrying about my children, my husband, and medical school, I was neglecting the child in me. I'd nod when he explained my dreams to me, as if I understood. I got that I worried about things in my life. I got that it interfered with my own peace and happiness. But I didn't see myself as a baby. Babies are pure and innocent and beautiful. That wasn't me. Martin came along once a week for couples' therapy, as he had with Jack. That was also useful. Dr. Jones helped us prepare for the possibility that we would move to a new city, which would involve settling the girls into new schools, the start of my medical residency, and Martin resuming an academic career.

I spent the rest of fourth year traveling for residency interviews, working in elective clerkships, and studying for medicine boards—the first step in the set of exams required to become a fully licensed physician. Martin and I agreed on three locations in which we would like to raise the girls and that would be good for our careers. I would need to go through the medical residency matching system, a computerized system for placing residents into programs that maximizes both the residency programs' picks and the applicants' wishes. Since we would be bound contractually to move to wherever I matched, we limited my requests to places where Martin received firm and timely promises of employment: the University of Washington in Seattle (his old job) and the University of California, San Diego. He could also remain at IBM Research in Yorktown Heights. I applied to match at residency programs at the University of Washington Medical School and Virginia Mason Hospital, both in Seattle, the University of California at San Diego, Scripps in San Diego, and New York Medical College, ranked in that order.

Dr. Jones served as my academic advisor, and neither of us saw a problem with continuing that after Jack's death. I wouldn't be entering psychiatry so there would not be a conflict with his treating me while I applied to New York Medical College's residency program. I met with him to go over the school's Dean's letter. This was the letter prepared for each student that summarized his or her performance during the two years of academic study and the two years of clinical rotations. An adjective describing me at the end of the letter caught my eye.

"It doesn't look very strong. Could it be changed?"

Dr. Jones smiled. "It's actually a code word. Medical schools aren't supposed to share student ranking. We use code words instead. Your code means that you ranked in the top 25 percent of the school's graduates."

My jaw dropped. I'd gone from a near-flunking status to a respectable rank. Decades later, I no longer recall the exact code word I'd been assigned. But I still feel the flush of realizing that not only was I going to graduate from medical school, I was doing so with some level of success.

I interviewed at the five programs. I didn't apply to New York programs other than New York Medical College because of our preference for Seattle. New York Medical was a pretty sure bet since I was a current student. The programs at Scripps and Virginia Mason were smaller, and therefore residents were required to take more frequent call, every third night. Spending the night away from home that often terrified me. Call every fourth night, as required by the other programs, would be bad enough. Every third night would mean I was on call or recovering from call all the time. Not good for a mommy. The program at University of California San Diego was a long shot—I only had an interview there because the director of New York Medical's internal medicine department called in a favor from a friend. My interview at University of Washington went very well, much better than the one prior to beginning medical school. One interviewer suggested I would be accepted there. The University of Washington was my top choice for several reasons. It was an outstanding program with excellent faculty. I'd have a chance to move into research after my residency. It had a primary care option, which involved more time in clinic and less in the hospital. This would mean doing more wellness and prevention care and less intensive care. It would also involve call only during six months of the year rather than yearlong as for other medicine programs. Seattle was Martin's top choice because he'd had an excellent experience in his old department at the university. And, probably most importantly, we knew from experience that Seattle was an excellent place to raise children.

I submitted my match choices in November and we waited anxiously for the results.

Match Day arrived on the third Friday in March 1989. This was the day that we would learn what internal medicine program selected me.

All of the fourth-year medical students and their loved ones gathered at noon in one large hall at the medical school. Martin came with me; this decision would affect him as much as it affected me. As a computer scientist, he had investigated the computer algorithm that would decide the rest of our lives. He had even talked with a computer scientist who wrote the textbook on this algorithm. He was satisfied that the match program would be fair for us, but it didn't reduce our anxiety about where we would be placed.

Several administrators and faculty were present as well. At one o'clock precisely, staff handed out sealed white envelopes. I asked Martin to open mine. The sound of ripping paper was deafening, followed by shouts and laughing and some quieter responses. The room swayed, and my hands tingled as I tried to see the piece of paper Martin held in his steady hand. It took a few seconds before I could read the print. Martin and I hugged. We'd be returning to Seattle. I'd matched at the University of Washington.

Chapter 27

JUNE 1989

Commencement ceremonies were scheduled for June 5. Martin and I received an invitation to an awards ceremony the day before commencement. The invitation stated that it was not for all students, so I should not share the information. Curious, we arranged a babysitter and went. Traffic was heavy; we arrived with only a few minutes to spare. The event was held in a large, white tent—the same tent that would be used the following day for commencement activities. After showing the invitation at the tent door, we were escorted to the front row. Our names were printed on two seats. We picked up the embossed programs that lay on our seats. Entitled, "Senior Honors Program and Reception Honoring the Class of 1989," the program listed approximately thirty-five awards. No student names were provided; the awardees would be a surprise. I recognized several school dignitaries on the stage—the President, Dean of Students, and chairs of several departments. Dr. Jones, who worked in administration, was also there.

The event began with speeches by the school President, a Monsignor, and the medical school dean. Each award would be described by a doctor, followed by the announcement of the awardee. Suddenly I realized the only reason I'd been invited was to receive an award. I was getting an award! I never got awards, not since high school when I'd been rewarded for being bookish and religious. Recognition of this type was for other people, particularly men. The ceremony progressed. As I heard the description of each award, I dismissed the possibility that I could be the recipient. Outstanding clinical skills? No. Excellence in anatomy? No way. Highest degree of compassion to patients? I was compassionate with patients but didn't shout about it. Outstanding contributions to the medical school? Nope. Alpha Omega Alpha Honor Medical Society citations? Not AOA material—those were the cream of the crop of medical students. Excellence in surgery? Not I. When only four awards remained, it occurred to me that I'd been invited by mistake. Oh great, I thought, a couple hours of babysitter costs just to watch others being lauded. Not that they didn't deserve it. I just had other priorities. Like taking care of the girls and helping them prepare to move away from New York. As I pondered, someone was talking about the Joan P. Liman, MD, award. The announcer stated that this award is presented to a graduate who, after endeavors in another career, has chosen to enter the field of Medicine and has achieved a distinguished academic record while serving the College community and student body of New York Medical College with dedication and enthusiasm. I heard my name called but didn't move. "It's for you, Anne," Martin whispered. "Go on up." Shaking, I stood and walked the four steps up to the stage, hoping my feet could support me without tripping. I walked to the center, shook hands with the smiling presenter, and took the plaque in my trembling hand. The presenter had me stop to pose for a picture, then let me slink back to my seat. Martin put his arm around me as I shivered.

At the conclusion of the program, Dr. Liman herself came over to congratulate me. I managed to thank her for the great honor and avoided saying I didn't deserve it. Martin and I talked with a few other students we recognized. When there was no one else nearby, Dr. Jones came over to congratulate me. He had nominated me for the award, he said. He really wanted to nominate me for the award that was in recognition for excellence despite difficult life circumstances, but he couldn't do that without violating doctor-patient confidentiality. I thanked him profusely but wondered how my life circumstances might have been depicted for an award. Most anxious student? Best test score while in a panic attack? Student with the most challenging extracurricular activities? Best psychotherapy patient? The possibilities seemed endless.

On the drive home, I alternated between pride and disbelief, leaning heavily to disbelief. I wouldn't announce my win to any of my friends. Only the other awardees knew that I'd been one of them. Although I secretly wanted to shout about my success with a megaphone out the car window as we drove, I didn't want to brag.

The following day—Graduation Day—was predicted to be warm and humid. Not a good hair day, but that didn't bother me too much. The cap and mortarboard I'd wear would squash my hair flat anyway. I wondered if "graduation mortarboard hat hair" was a term. The gown worried me more. Its cheap black material had no air flow. I was guaranteed to sweat from the anxiety of it all, and the wetness wouldn't evaporate.

Some of my family came to the ceremony—Martin, the girls, my mother and aunt, and Martin's mother. My father had said congratulations when I told him I'd graduate soon. He expressed no interest in attending.

My mother looked uncomfortable—I suspected she didn't like me getting all of the attention. Margie beamed with pride. My mother-in-law was in tears, and they were not tears of joy. She blamed me for our decision to return to Seattle.

The ceremony involved more speeches and students receiving diplomas one at a time (Martin whooped when I collected mine). Then, with one voice, the graduates recited the Hippocratic Oath. The version printed in our yearbook included dated material. It assumes the physician is a man, swears by Apollo and other gods and goddesses, and promises to financially support his teachers. But in the oath, we practitioners vowed to follow high ethical standards and that is as relevant today as it was in ancient Greece. Following this, we enjoyed champagne and white sheet cake, underscoring physicians' lack of nutritional knowledge. I overindulged in both.

Pictures from that day show me smiling in cap and gown and holding my diploma in front of me: alone, with the girls, with Martin, with Martin and the girls, with my mother and aunt, with Martin's mother. Then there were pictures of Rachel in cap and gown and holding the diploma, and pictures of Cassie in cap and gown and holding the diploma. While I hoped my girls could achieve their own dreams, I wanted them to have an easier path than I'd had. I wished success without angst for them.

On my personal page in the New York Medical College yearbook, I selected a quote from Bertolt Brecht's *Jungle of Cities*: "It isn't important to come out on top; what matters is to be the one who comes out alive." While I wasn't at the absolute top of my graduating medical school class, I was good enough, and I was very much alive. My loved ones and healers had kept me alive and well.

I celebrated two milestones that day. The obvious one was that I had transitioned from student to doctor. I now had the MD—Medical Doctor—initials behind my name. I was a real doctor. I had endured four years of grueling study, work, and worry. I'd entered the process insecure and with the belief that becoming a doctor would cure me of my low self-esteem. I emerged highly educated, trained to heal, and deeply appreciative of what doctors need to know to do their jobs. Soon I'd embark on more training. I was ready.

The second milestone was the completion of almost four years of therapy. I went into that treatment in a panic, underwent a remodeling of how I process emotions, and finished as a calmer person more in touch with her feelings. Yet, there'd be no parchment for this graduation, no new initials behind my name. While there was no advanced therapy program for me to move into, I'd need to continue what Jack and Dr. Jones had taught me. Just as doctors are required to receive continuing medical education throughout their careers, I would need to keep practicing feeling the feelings.

Martin and I changed as a couple as a result of our therapy. We began to share our thoughts and feelings. We learned more about each other, and about ourselves, in the process. We have been married now for forty-four years; Martin tells me he loves me almost every day.

The girls also benefited from our therapy, I hope. Certainly, a relaxed mom made a better mom. We paid more attention to our rigid parenting and tried to work on that. The girls might have wished we'd done more, but at least we did some.

We parted ways with the grandparents and drove on to the hotel we'd stay in that night before flying the following morning to Seattle. The next phase of our lives was about to begin.

Epilogue

I began medical school surrounded by dead bodies. I finished surrounded by the living—my vibrant family, friends, colleagues, and patients. Medicine is about the living. It's about helping people feel the best they can with the bodies they have.

For several years, I practiced medicine in a low-income clinic. My goal was to help patients lead more healthy, satisfied lives with the bodies they were given. There was the middle-aged man originally from Mexico whose cholesterol was a little higher than normal. We reviewed his diet choices, I gave him tips on what foods to increase and decrease, and his cholesterol dropped significantly. There was the sixty-year-old Asian-American woman with hypertension. While her blood pressure was controlled well with her three medications, she wanted to do more. I told her that exercise can help lower blood pressure and convinced her to begin a walking program. She walked faithfully every day, which lowered her blood pressure enough that we were able to discontinue her most expensive medication. Unfortunately, she stopped exercising when her boyfriend—her walking buddy—died. There was the fifty-five-year-old white bachelor with diabetes, hypertension, heart disease, hip pain, and stomach problems. He wouldn't change his diet, couldn't exercise because of pain, and skipped his medications periodically. He didn't do well. There was the elderly African-American grandmother who couldn't make it to some of her appointments with me because she had to babysit her grandchildren. Her daughters—employed in low-income jobs—faced pay cuts or being fired if they missed time from work.

These patients taught me that following doctors' advice might be difficult but could succeed if the conditions were right. Many patients could not afford the medications I prescribed; I'd have to find lower-priced alternatives or scrounge in the clinic drug cabinet for free samples. Family duties interfered with the best intentions of many patients and often their health suffered. I came to realize that I could have more effect conducting research in populations, to discover what types of lifestyles, medications, and health strategies could prevent the diseases that plagued my patients.

Now, as a researcher who studies health in clinical trials and large populations, I'm surrounded by multitudes of live bodies and the promise of better lives.

I recall with gratitude all the people who helped me learn to be a doctor: Martin, our daughters, my brilliant caring attendings, dozens of interns and residents, fellow medical students, Jack, Dr. Jones, and, always, the patients. My computer's thesaurus gives me synonyms for "patient," including: enduring, persistent, persevering, easy-going, tolerant, long-suffering, serene, unflappable, imperturbable, good-natured, understanding, uncomplaining, unwearied. These descriptions are so appropriate to the many patients who allowed me to learn how to doctor.

Martin and I keep a wind chime on our back porch. Made of aluminum, it has six vertical tubes of varying length. I bought it in a garden store after returning to Yorktown Heights two months after Jack's death. It has moved with us to three different homes. The wind chime hangs sheltered from the weather, but when a gust hits, it tinkles and sings. Jack was like our wind chime, showing me the beauty that can arise in the midst of a tempest. Jack is silent now, dead for over thirty years. But every once in a while, I recall his words, as beautiful as a wind chime's song: *You'll be okay, you can do it.*

PHOTO CREDITS

p. 113: Courtesy of Sruti Ram

p. 131: Courtesy of Joy Lofstrand

p. 132: Courtesy of Joy Lofstrand

p. 133: Courtesy of Judi Purcell

p. 149: Courtesy of Sruti Ram

p. 156: Courtesy of Neem Karoli Baba Ashram

p. 159: Courtesy of Sruti Ram

p. 165: Courtesy of Sruti Ram

p. 168: By Mary Bloom, courtesy of Sruti Ram

p. 175: By Rasa Partin, courtesy of Ishwari L. Keller

p. 177: By Cynthia DelConte, courtesy of Ishwari L. Keller

p. 188: Courtesy of Sruti Ram

p. 191: By Rasa Partin, courtesy of Ishwari L. Keller

ABOUT THE AUTHOR

Sruti Ram was born as George Palmer on July 21, 1943, the second son to Italian-American parents in the Pelham section of the Bronx in New York City. At age thirteen, after his father died, Sruti Ram and his mother moved to Riverdale, where he attended Catholic school, joined a Gregorian choir, and sang doo-wop. After graduating from high school, he began a hairdressing career, catering to many rock 'n' roll figures, that would last fifty-five years.

But as a young adult, Sruti Ram left his jetsetter lifestyle to practice meditation and yoga and seek his higher purpose in life. He traveled extensively throughout India and became a devotee of Neem Karoli Baba; and he studied with Ram Dass, acting for many years as meditation master at Ram Dass's retreats and, during the mid-1970s, running two residences of Ram Dass students in Queens, New York. Later, Sruti Ram moved to Woodstock, New York, where he reestablished his hairdressing business and led a kirtan and bhakti devotional yoga group.

Sruti Ram formed SRI Kirtan with singer and musician Ishwari Keller in 2004, traveling throughout the United States and India to lead kirtans and record several CDs. He became a beacon of light for many fellow spiritual seekers and formed an extended family around the world. Although many members of Sruti Ram's generation looked to the East for spiritual awakening, few were as passionate or as dedicated as he was regarding practicing love for all fellow beings.

Sruti Ram died on December 16, 2020, in Kingston, New York, of complications due to COVID-19.